*The*
# Compassion
*of*
# Missions

*Jim Lo*

Wesleyan Publishing House
Indianapolis, Indiana

Copyright © 2000 by Wesleyan Publishing House
All Rights Reserved
Published by Wesleyan Publishing House
Indianapolis, Indiana 46250
Printed in the United States of America
ISBN 0-89827-212-2

All rights reserved. No part of this publication may be reproduced, stored in a retrieval system, or transmitted in any form or by any means—electronic, mechanical, photocopy, recording or any other—except for brief quotations in printed reviews without the prior written permission of the publisher.

# Table of Contents

The Compassion of Missions ......... 5

Com(e) ............................ 19

Compass ........................... 51

Passion ........................... 71

Pass-i'-on ......................... 85

Sí ................................ 95

# the Compassion of Missions

Jethro, Albert, and Temba were young men from Zimbabwe who had attended our Bible school in Swaziland. With great academic success they completed their studies. They were ranked number one, two, and three in their graduating class. The church in Zimbabwe was excitedly awaiting their return. Weeks before the three were to return to Zimbabwe, the Zimbabwean believers spent hours discussing what they could do to welcome home their returning "heroes." Parties were planned by many of the churches. Gifts were gathered to bestow upon them.

But after a while, the churches in Zimbabwe began to recognize that things were not going well. Jethro, Temba, and Albert began to say things that revealed what was really within their hearts.

"We want more money if you expect us to continue to pastor!"

"Don't expect us to live near the church. We don't want to be bothered by people knocking on our door."

"We will only work so many hours a week. Anything after that is our time . . . to be used as we want."

Within one year, each of these young men who had prepared for the ministry crossed illegally over the border into South Africa. They went there to find employment that would pay them more than they could receive by being pastors. I was truly hurt by their exodus. For weeks I felt guilty. I kept thinking to myself,

"Perhaps we should have given them a bigger salary," or
"Perhaps we should have provided not only a house but also nice furniture," or
"Perhaps we were expecting too much from them."

I shared these thoughts with a wise and faithful Zimbabwean Christian.

After allowing me time to share my feelings, he stated, "The salaries that the young men were receiving were better than what the majority of Zimbabweans receive. The manzes (parsonages) provided them by the church were very adequate for them to live comfortably. The real problem was not money, or housing, or the work hours. The real problem was that they did not love enough. Their lack of compassion for God and for the lost is the real reason why they left!"

### Compassion at work.

Now, I would not want you to think that all our stories about our Bible graduates end on such a negative note. Daniel Cossa attended Bible school at the same time as Jethro, Temba, and Albert. As graduation day approached, Daniel knew that he was to return to Mozambique. This was not an exciting prospect. Mozambique was going through a civil war that had already lasted over twenty years. The country had been devastated by the internal conflict among its citizens. Daniel knew that returning to Mozambique would be a bleak situation. Mozambique was a land where food was scarce. He had received reports from relatives still living in Mozambique that the majority of the people were eating only one meal a day. Many were only able to find enough food to eat one meal every two or three days.

Mozambique, at that time, was also a land where there had been many killings. News of Wesleyan pastors being murdered by dissident forces regularly reached the ears of those living in Swaziland. Often times there was no real reason for the killing of these pastors. They were tortured and shot to death for the sadistic pleasure of some over-zealous soldier.

*The Compassion of Missions*

*Daniel and Lydia Cossa with family*

The people of Mozambique understand the realities of what persecution is all about.

The Mozambican church was also too poor to provide an adequate salary for those involved in full-time ministry. There was no promise of any type of salary for the Cossas if they were to go back to preach.

For weeks leading up to graduation, Daniel struggled with knowing what to do. During his years studying at the Bible school, he had been student pastoring one of the village churches. The people of his congregation loved and appreciated Daniel, his wife, and children. They sensed God's anointing upon his preaching and ministry. They tried to persuade him and his family to stay on as their pastoral family even after graduation.

The offer was very tempting for the Cossas. Remaining in Swaziland would mean adequate food supplies, a regular salary from the church, and safety from bodily harm. Weekly, different members of the church would approach the Cossas, encouraging them to stay.

*The Compassion of Missions*

"Be our pastor. We will take good care of you. What is there in Mozambique for you to go back to?"

"It's safe here in Swaziland. There are no landmines here. There is no war here. We have peace. Think about your family. It would be better for you to stay here with us . . . at least until there is no more fighting in Mozambique."

For a brief time Daniel seriously considered the offer made to him by the Christians from the village church in Swaziland. Swaziland did seem to be a much better place to live, raise a family, and minister than Mozambique. It would be better for him, his career, and for his wife and children.

One night he drew his wife aside to tell her about his decision to remain in Swaziland. He thought his news would be received with great joy. Instead, his wife Lydia encouraged him to rethink his decision. She asked him, "Have you fasted and prayed about this decision?"

Daniel had to confess that he had not. His decision had been based on what he thought was best for him and his family. He had not really been concerned about what was best for the kingdom of God. Lydia then proposed that they both spend time seeking the will of God. For days they fasted and sought for God's plan for their lives.

They finally reached the conclusion that God would be pleased for them to return to Mozambique to minister. Many of the Swazis continued to try to persuade them to change their minds. "It doesn't make sense for you to return to Mozambique when you can have it so good here." Again and again people said to them, "You are crazy to not take advantage of this opportunity to stay in Swaziland where life is so much more comfortable."

The Cossas' reply was, "Our aim in life is not to be comfortable but to be obedient to our Lord."

They held firm to their decision to return to war-torn Mozambique. Once they knew where God wanted them, nothing and nobody could deter them from following God's will for their lives. Not even the bleakness of the situation

*The Compassion of Missions*

could discourage Daniel and Lydia. They were returning to their people. The Cossas understood the suffering and distress of their Mozambican brothers and sisters. Their desire was to return home and be instruments that God would use to alleviate the spiritual suffering.

The Cossas were assigned a congregation that numbered less than twenty in a place called Mafalala. There was no beautiful church building for them to worship in. In fact, there was no building at all. Those who came for worship sat upon large rocks or upon the ground. During hot, sunny days, the people sought the shade of trees for relief from the heat.

One could wonder, what chance did the Cossas have of ever pastoring a strong church? The initial number of attendees to their church was small. There was no building for them to worship in. There was no salary to adequately supply the needs of their family. There was no money to help the church reach higher levels. The odds were totally against them.

**"Our aim in life is not to be comfortable but to be obedient to the Lord."**

But within a short period of time after their arrival, the attendance of the church began to grow and it continued to grow. I have personally been privileged to preach and teach at their church when over 250 individuals were gathered to worship the King of kings. When I asked some of the people what was the cause for the growth, the most frequent answer was, "We know the Cossas love God. And because they love God, they are able to really love us. People are attracted to love!" The church in Mafalala has been able to grow in numbers and spiritual maturity because Daniel and Lydia recognized that church work is more than just a job but is a ministry of compassion.

## Compassion defined.

The Oxford English dictionary defines compassion as "the feeling or emotion when a person is moved by the suffering or distress of another . . . and the desire to relieve it."

Compassion must be an integral part of missions. The apostle Paul wrote in Romans 10:1 that "my heart's desire . . . is that they may be saved." Being filled with compassion causes one to view missions, or any ministry one does for the Lord,

- not just as a job or an unpleasant chore,
  but as a God-ordained task;
- not just as an eight-to-five assignment,
  but as a 24-hour-a-day calling;
- not just as a source for payment,
  but as a way to bring glory to the Father, Son, and Holy Ghost.

## Personalizing compassion.

I would love to say that I have mastered the understanding and practice of compassion. But like many believers, I am continually growing in this area.

The Wesleyan Church in Zimbabwe was planting a church in the township of Magwegwe West. The church planting pastor asked if I would be willing to speak to his small, yet growing congregation. Enthusiastically I accepted his invitation.

Early Sunday morning, Roxy, the boys, and I got into our car and made our way to the new church plant. Upon arriving at the address we were given, we noticed that people were already gathering for worship. There was no beautiful church building for us to worship in. Instead, the people were meeting in the home of a believer who had opened her house to The Wesleyan Church.

Now you must get the full picture of this house. It was nothing like the houses you and I live in. The homes in African townships tend to be very small. One visiting American aptly

*The Compassion of Missions*

described them as "matchboxes." The rooms are tiny. But the smallness of space did not deter the people from meeting on Sunday mornings. Over thirty bodies were tightly crammed into two small rooms. Since there were no pews or chairs, we were all seated upon the hard cement floor. Those who could not squeeze themselves into the two rooms sat outside in the hot sun, still fully participating in the worship service.

African worship services tend to be long. I have participated in worship services in Zimbabwe that lasted for nearly seven hours. The average length for a worship service tends to be around two or three hours long. But I usually do not mind the lengthiness of the services. The joy of worshipping God and fellowshipping with other believers always has a way of dimming the discomforts we may be experiencing. That morning at Magwegwe West, the worship service lasted for approximately two hours. The music was exceptionally good. As the African believers sang, they began

*Church in Magwegwe West*

*The Compassion of Missions*

to sway to the beat of the music. Before long some stood up, dancing demonstratively before the Lord. Worship in Africa can be both fun and inspirational.

After the service, the pastor asked if I would be willing to go with him and pray for someone who was ill in the community. Though my stomach was growling from hunger, I decided that the right thing for me to do was to go with him.

Within a short time we arrived at our destination. We walked up the steps into the house. Pastor Ndebele greeted the family and made the appropriate introductions. Once that was over we were ushered into the bedroom.

The bedroom was dark. Though it was a warm day outside, the windows were tightly closed. Dark, worn drapes prevented the light of the sun to from entering. Many of the Shona tribe of Zimbabwe are superstitious. They are fearful that when people are ill, they are susceptible to having their spirits taken away from them by evil spirits. With the windows closed and draped, one's spirit would be confined within the boundaries of the four walls if it were to leave a person. It took a few moments for my eyes to adjust to the darkness after being outside where the sun was shining brightly. Gradually I was able to make out the scene before me.

A bed took up most of the space in the room. Seated upright in the bed was an old woman. Her clothing was ragged and wrinkled. Her hair was unkept. Her eyes were sunken and her skin hung from her body. It did not take much intelligence to recognize that she was the one we had come to pray for. On the right side of the bed was a wooden chair which had seen better days. Seated upon the chair was a young man who must have been in his early twenties. His face was buried in his hands. His shoulders were moving up and down as he silently cried. Since I was there to pray for the sick, I lifted my hands and placed them on the head of the sick woman.

In the IsiNdebele language I prayed, "Dear Lord, please be with "gogo" (grandmother). Do your will in this situation. As the all powerful God, I know that you can touch this "gogo"

*The Compassion of Missions*

physically. But Lord, even more important, please speak to her spirit . . . help her to understand the wonder of your salvation. And Lord, please be with her son who is in such agony because of this grandmother's sickness. . . . Amen."

Even before I could completely articulate my closing "Amen," the old woman shrieked, and with tears of anger rolling down her sunken cheeks, cried out, "I am not a gogo! And that is not my son. That is my husband!"

Now I had been on African soil long enough to know that it was not customary for a young man to marry an old woman. I was confused. My look of helplessness and embarrassment moved Pastor Ndebele to action. He moved out of the room and began to converse with the family again. I stood awkwardly in the room with the old woman and young man. Thick silence filled the room. Each one of us was deep in our own thoughts, not making any connection with the other people in the room. The old woman was rhythmically rocking

*The Compassion of Missions*

back and forth on the bed. The young man was still silently crying. I stood as still as I could, not wanting any movement to draw attention to myself. I was fearful of another emotional outbreak. It seemed like ages before Pastor Ndebele came back into the room.

When he finally came back to rescue me, he stated, "Umfundisi, this woman has the 'wasting away disease.' She is not a gogo. She is only around twenty years old. And she was telling the truth. That is not her son seated over there. That is her husband!"

There have been many ways in which AIDS has been described around the world. Because AIDS physically eats away at a person, the Africans call it the wasting away disease. I was shocked and disgusted. No longer was I concerned about the health of the sick "gogo." I was concerned about my own health. All I could think was "I just touched a person with AIDS!"

I did not want to stay in the confines of that germ-infested room any longer than I had to. All I could think about were the germs that were floating around the room. I needed fresh air. Rudely I blurted, "Let's get out of here!" and without following proper African etiquette, hurriedly walked out of the house to get to my car.

I have a bad habit of chewing my nails. But that day I never once put my fingers close to my mouth. I did not want the AIDS "bugs" to enter my body. (This shows my ignorance concerning how a person could contract the HIV virus.)

When I and my family finally arrived back home, I went directly to the kitchen sink and turned the hot water faucet on. I wanted the water to be as hot as possible since I had heard that heat killed germs. On the side of the sink was a bottle of liquid soap. Liquid soap was very expensive to buy in Zimbabwe. But that did not matter to me at the moment. All I could think about was using as much of it as possible in order to get my hands clean. I must have used half a bottle in one washing, much to the disgust of my wife Roxy. But I was beyond worrying about how she was feeling. I was more concerned about not dying. By the end of the day my hands were red and sore because I had probably washed them at least twenty times.

As night began to settle in, I took my Bible to have my personal devotions. But as I opened my Bible and began to read, my mind was not able to stay focused on the printed words. After a few failed attempts to grasp what the Bible was trying to say to me, I closed it, shut my eyes, and began to pray. Yet even while I was praying, I did not feel as if I were making intimate contact with God. My speeding, worrying mind was blocking the flow of communication. I decided that I would just quiet myself and allow the Lord to speak to me.

Have you ever heard God speaking to you? That night I felt God speaking to me. It was not in a loud, deep voice. In fact it was not even an audible voice. I cannot explain it. But I knew that as I was sitting there, with my Bible closed upon my lap, God was speaking to my spirit. The conversation He and I began to have with one another went something like this.

"Jim, you have a problem."

"What do you mean, Lord?"

"You call yourself a missionary. But you don't have the heart of a missionary."

"What do you mean Lord? I am trying to be obedient. Wasn't I making a big sacrifice when I decided to leave the comforts of America to come to Africa? And don't I regularly visit the churches to encourage them by my preaching and teaching? And Lord, don't you see the times when I have walked miles to reach a village church to worship with them? And Lord, don't you see the many hours that I have spent learning the African language in order for me to be able to communicate with them?"

"What about your actions today, Jim?"

"But Lord, you don't understand. The lady had AIDS. I could have gotten it. The final outcome would have been death. If I were to die, what use would I be to You then?"

"Jim, I *do* understand. Don't you remember what you were before you accepted my Son, Jesus, as your Savior? You were

*The Compassion of Missions*

filthy with the disease of sin. Yet Jesus was willing to touch and love you. Where would you be if Jesus had avoided you because He did not want to become dirty with sin?

"Jesus' concern was not for himself. His concern was for the spiritual well-being of mankind. His compassion for the human race made him willing to be incarnated and to be vulnerable and exposed to the ills of this world. And it eventually led *Him* to the cross! This must be the attitude of missionaries. This must be your attitude. Your concern must not be for your own personal protection and comfort. If you truly love Me, you will want to be filled with a compassion for the lost which will move you out into a world where there will be risks of disease and suffering and discomfort."

> "You call yourself a missionary. But you don't have the heart of a missionary."

That night the chair I had been sitting on became an altar for me as I asked for God's forgiveness. He was correct. I was more concerned for my own safety than for the welfare of other people. That night I told God that I did not want to just be a missionary in name only. With a humbled heart, I asked God to help me to be the type of missionary that He would be pleased with.

Beloved, we need to be so consumed with His love that we will be willing to compassionately serve others even if it means that we have to move beyond our comfort zones.

**The parts of compassion.**

There was a game I learned to play while attending Mount Vernon Primary School in New Jersey. The teacher would think of a big word. Once she had one she would write it on the blackboard.

She would then turn around, face the class, and give us students the rules for playing the game. We were to look at the

16

*The Compassion of Missions*

big word, and then from its letters write down how many little words we could come up with. In a way, that is what I am going to be doing in the following pages with the word *compassion*.

Discovering little words in a big word reminds me of the biology class I took while I was in high school. Biology was one of my favorite classes. I had heard from upper classmen that it was the grossest class a person could take in high school. And I was not disappointed.

Upon entering the laboratory on the first day, my eyes became riveted to the many jars of specimens that sat upon the shelves which lined the walls. There were fetuses of dogs, cats, pigs, and even an elephant. In one larger jar was a medium-sized monkey.

The prospect of dissecting animals fascinated me. Visions of being like Dr. Kildaire or Dr. Marcus Welby, two famous television medical men, filled my mind. To be like Dr. Frankenstein was even more appealing. (I was a little strange when I was in high school.) Being called Dr. Jim Lo, M.D., sounded rather appealing to me.

After we had impatiently studied the structures of plant life for a few weeks, our teacher announced one Friday that we

17

would begin studying animal life and enter into the dissecting phase of the class. The boys of the class gave a hearty cheer. The girls in the class gave a pitiful groan.

Monday morning, I was so excited that my hands were actually shaking at the prospect of cutting something up. Once we were all seated, our biology teacher gave us instructions. We were going to dissect an earthworm. He then walked around to each lab station and with large tweezers, placed an earthworm on the small tray in front of each student.

Now, if you have never dissected an earthworm, you have not missed all that much. For me it was a great disappointment! I spent a large portion of the class period trying to determine which side of the worm was up and which side was down.

It was only towards the latter part of the semester that we began dissecting more interesting specimens. What I enjoyed dissecting the most was a stiff cat that my lab partner and I nicknamed "Stiffy." To dissect a kitty cat was the ultimate thing to do for a bunch of immature freshmen.

Now you are probably wondering why I told you such a stupid story. The reason our teacher had us dissect different types of animals was to help us understand the makeup of animals. I am proposing that we dissect the word *compassion* to better understand its different aspects and components, to see what parts make up the whole.

# Com(e)

T he first little word I see in *compassion* is the word *come*.

### C-o-m-p-a-s-s-i-o-n

I can see all the red lights. You are thinking to yourself, "Jim doesn't know how to spell." You must understand that I was not the best speller in grade school. For that matter, I'm not all that great of a speller even today. My wife Roxy regularly reads what I write to correct any spelling mistakes that I may have. So it's *come* without the "e", but I think you get the idea.

Part of compassion is introducing others to God. We want them to come to . . .

The Great *Unkulunkulu*,
The Majestic Lord, *Nkosi*,
The Sacrificial Redeemer, *Umhlengi*,
The One and Only Savior, *Umsindisi*.

The Bible resounds with the call to come. The disciple Philip urged Nathanael to "come and see" Jesus. Andrew also persuaded his brother Peter to come and see.

And today, this is what we must tell the world to do. With upheaval, violence and rapid change all over the world, people are looking for answers. The task of missions is to urge people to "come and see" Jesus Christ, to direct them to the Rock of stability. We must boldly shout forth the words, "Come to Jesus!"

### Christ is the end.

South African children often compliment a person by saying, "That person is the end!" They mean that the individual they are talking about is cool. Or wonderful. Or the solution to a problem they are having.

Notice with me how the apostle Paul describes Christ in Romans 10:4. He writes, "Christ is the end." This is the reason why we need to tell people to come to Christ. He is the end. He is cool. He is wonderful. He is the solution to all of mankind's physical, emotional, and spiritual needs. Christ is the end because what He offers is eternal.

The world would have us seek after many different earthly things to find peace, joy, and fulfillment. But the things of this world are not lasting. They cannot provide us with lasting satisfaction. Only Jesus Christ can do that.

### Mr. Potato Head.

I began to learn the truth of how fleeting the things of this world are when I was very young. My ninth birthday was quickly approaching. While Christmas is my favorite day of the year, my birthday is a close second. I love getting presents.

When my mom asked me what I wanted for my birthday, I would proceed to give her my list. "How about a Tonka truck . . . or a water gun . . . or a Freddy Flintstone car . . . or . . ."

Every time I saw a toy advertised on television, I felt that I could not be happy until I had that toy for my own. Then one day I saw a commercial advertising Mr. Potato Head. "Buy a Mr. Potato Head. Take him with you wherever you go. Show him to your friends. You will be the rave among your friends."

"Mom, I want a Mr. Potato Head. If you buy him for me, I will never ask you for anything else!" (Childhood promises.)

On the day of my birthday, I received many gifts. My brother Tom gave me a water gun to squirt girls. Bill gave me a yo-yo that whistled as it went up and down the string. And my mom got me a Mr. Potato Head. Boy, was I a happy lad!

When I was a child, Mr. Potato Head didn't come with a plastic head but needed a real potato. It's too bad young people today miss the fun of having to search for a large potato in a brown potato bag, washing the potato, and then sticking its anatomical parts on. My Mr. Potato Head was soooo cool. He had two large, blue eyes, a pudgy brown nose, bright red "kissing" lips, a polka-dotted bow tie, a tiny black derby hat, two large ears (that my brothers said resembled my ears), and a pair of hands and a pair of feet.

I loved my Mr. Potato Head. He sat on the table near me during meal times. For every bite I ate, I also gave my new "friend" a bite to eat. When I took a bubble bath, Mr. Potato Head also got a soaking. When I went to bed, Mr. Potato Head accompanied me. There was much comfort in knowing that Mr. Potato Head was there to watch over me and protect me from any unfriendly intruders.

The next morning, with Mr. Potato Head cradled in my arms, I arrived at the kitchen table for breakfast. Upon seeing

*The Compassion of Missions*

what I was carrying, my mom asked me what I was planning to do with him. "Mom, I want to show off Mr. Potato Head to my friends."

My mom gave a look that said, "Has my son gone nuts? There is no way I want the world to know that my son has gone soft in the head!"

"Jim, you march yourself right back to your room and leave Mr. Potato Head here at home. What will people think if you walk around with him? Other children have dogs or cats or gold fish . . . my son has to have a potato."

Glum and grumbling, I went back to my room. What was I going to do with my new friend? Wouldn't he get lonely without me around all day? What could I do to help him have a pleasant day in such an unpleasant situation?

Then a wonderful idea dawned on me. I would place Mr. Potato Head on my windowsill so that he could get plenty of sunlight and amuse himself by looking outside to see the activities of the neighborhood. As I left him to go to school, I gave him a good-bye kiss, smack on his red lips. I then placed him on the windowsill.

Now you must understand that I was a very sloppy child. My room always had mountain-high piles of clothing scattered throughout the room. It was rare that one could locate clear flooring, since it was typically recarpeted with school books, comic books, shoes, blankets and sheets, candy wrappers and whatever else your imagination can come up with.

After returning from school, I decided that it would take too much effort to try to crawl through and over the obstacles in my room to retrieve Mr. Potato Head. I decided I would leave him standing on the windowsill until I had time to clear a path to get to him. I was certain that he would not mind. He was comfortable enough. Besides, there was always some kind of activity going on in the neighborhood to keep his attention.

My room had a way of staying a mess for weeks on end. In my heart I had great intentions of keeping it clean and straightened-up. But my intentions never seemed to become

*Com(e)*

reality. Thus, weeks passed before I saw my friend, standing lonely on the windowsill, again. An interesting transformation had taken place though. No longer was he wrinkle-free and young. The weeks of standing in the sun had shriveled him up . . . he was old and wrinkly . . . and the fungus made him look as if he had also grown a greenish beard.

You are probably wondering why I recounted this story to you. Allow me to explain. I told my mom that if she would buy me Mr. Potato Head, I would never ask her for anything else again since he would make me happy and content for the rest of my life. How wrong I was. Mr. Potato Head did not and could not provide me with lasting happiness. He did not have eternal value. In only a few weeks he had become just a mushy potato. Too often people think that the things of this world will give them lasting happiness. This is not true. Jesus Christ said,

*Do not store up for yourselves treasures on earth, where moth and rust destroy, and where thieves break in and steal. But store up for yourselves treasures in heaven, where moth and rust do not destroy, and where thieves do not break in and steal.* (Matthew 6:19-20). <u>Our treasure must be Jesus Christ</u>.

*The Compassion of Missions*

This past Christmas I celebrated my twenty-sixth spiritual birthday. I can honestly testify that Christ has filled me with lasting joy and inner contentment. With unwavering assurance, I know that I am destined for an eternal home in heaven. Coming to Jesus at the age of nineteen was the best thing I have ever done.

## Bondage keeps many from coming.

Bondage of many different types keeps people around the world today from coming to Christ. I have seen what the bondage of superstitious fear can do to people.

One day I was doing visitation with Rev. William Selamalela in a Sotho village. As we walked around the living areas of the villagers, I noticed that near the entrance of many family huts a hole had been dug out. Out of curiosity I asked William what the holes in the ground were for.

"Umfundisi Jim, those holes are where the Sothos pour their beer as an offering to evil spirits. Many people in Africa do this as the means of appeasing the spirits so that they will not do the people any harm."

Though I am not African, my oriental background allowed me to understand what Pastor William was telling me. As a small child, I lived in Hong Kong where people today still worship their ancestral spirits. Before each evening meal, many families bow down before a large picture of one of their ancestors and ask for a blessing. A place is set at the meal table where no living person is allowed to sit because it is reserved for the ancestral spirits.

In some tribal societies, sharp razors are used to cut designs onto the bodies and faces of young men and women in order to leave symbolic scars. The belief is that the scars will ward off any spirits that may seek to do harm to the person or his or her family.

Many Cambodians believe that sickness is caused by supernatural entities. In order to protect their children from these menacing spirits, parents go to the witch doctor to ask for help.

*Com(e)*

After a price has been negotiated and money exchanged, the *doctor* proceeds to do his work. Leaving the parents and infant child, the witch doctor enters the thick jungles of Cambodia in search of the bettlenut tree. Once it has been located, the witch doctor climbs its limbs and plucks off some of its leaves.

Arriving back at his *office*, the witch doctor takes the bettlenut leaves and folds them in a particular and secretive way. It is believed that the manner in which the leaves are folded gives them supernatural medicinal powers. The witch doctor then places a few of the leaves in his mouth and sucks on them until a large amount of yellow spittle is formed. The child is then stripped naked and the witch doctor proceeds to spit the yellow fluid all over the child. The liquid slowly runs down the child's body, leaving a yellow film as it dries. The parents are told not to wash this film off. To do so would mean that the child will no longer be protected.

When you and I hear about this form of protection, we may think to ourselves, "How gross. That is disgusting. Why would any one do something like that?" But this is what people will do when they are in bondage to superstitious fear.

*The Compassion of Missions*

This bondage of superstition was also demonstrated to me by something that took place in a small village in one of the northeast provinces of Cambodia. An old man of the village was leading one of his oxen to the slaughterhouse. As the man walked slowly down the dirt path, he stopped to chat with a man who had a festering sore on one of his legs. As the two men were talking, the ox began to lick the open sore. According to reports, with each stroke of the ox's tongue, the man's sore began to disappear. When the owner of the ox saw this, the plan of killing it was no longer part of his thinking.

People from the village began to deify this "magical" animal. It was placed in the center of the open air market. Those who were sick traveled many miles to pray in the presence of the god-ox and burn incense to it. Some stood close to its mouth in hopes of being licked. Others got on their knees and crawled under its belly to benefit from its magical powers of healing.

Before long someone came up with a better idea. If crawling under the belly of the ox could bring healing, what would

*Com(e)*

happen if part of the animal could be ingested? What could one ingest of the ox without killing it? The answer was simple. The owners of the ox obtained containers to collect its urine and dung. Signs were put up advertising the cost. People began paying hard earned money to buy the unconventional medicine. It was quite a sight to watch people drinking the ox's urine and

chewing or smoking its dung. The ox became world wide news. CNN sent in a crew of news correspondents to report about it. All I could think to myself was, "What people will do when they are caught in the bondage of superstition."

People today are experiencing many other forms of bondage as well. The sad consequences of sexual immorality were very evident in Cambodia when I was ministering there. The city of Phnom Phen reportedly has over 30,000 prostitutes. Girls under the age of twelve are selling their bodies. Tourists from all over the world enter Cambodia to "get some flesh." When one gets a room at a hotel, one of the questions asked is, "Do you want a girl for the night?"

Pornography is destroying the lives of many people. One pastor shared with me how pornography had affected the attendance at his church. A man who had been a faithful member decided to get his televisions hooked up to cable. With no boundaries set, he began to view questionable programs. Before long he was watching pornographic films. He became so caught up with watching 'X' and 'R' rated shows, he no longer had time to attend church. Once he stopped going, his wife and children stopped going. Eventually, the embarrassment of what he was doing caused his extended family to also stop attending church.

Young people regularly confess to being caught in the destructive web of pornography. One young man shared, "I didn't mean for it to go this far. At first I thought I could handle and control what I was viewing. I thought I was mature. But now I know that I was wrong. I am losing control. I know that as a Christian I should not be looking at such things . . . but it is almost as if something else is controlling me . . . forcing me to look at what I do not want to look at. My spiritual life is not what it should be. . . ."

There is also the bondage of consumerism. I have noticed that many in America are bound by the chains of wanting to buy more and more. But in order to buy more, they have to work longer hours. By working longer hours they are forced to neglect spending time with their families and friends. One man stated, "I come home so exhausted that all I want to do is drop into my recliner and vegetate. I have no energy to talk with my wife or play with my children. I put my brain in neutral and just watch television." There is more to life than this!

**Crying to God for help.**

The Old Testament tells the story of Gideon. For seven years the Midianites had been oppressing the Israelite nation. The Israelites had reached an emotional limit. They did not feel as if they could take any more. They were oppressed prisoners, bound by the heavy chains of their enemies.

*Com(e)*

Because the bondage of oppression had become too heavy for the Israelites to bear any longer, they began to cry out to God for His help. This is a very important truth for us to understand. The account of Gideon teaches us that help is not to be found . . .
    in man alone,
    or methods alone,
    or money alone.
    Help is to be found in God, the Master.

## Man alone is not the answer.

After years of being persecuted by the Midianites, the Israelites began to pray to God for His help. The Lord answered the cries of the people. He raised up a prophet for them in the form of Gideon. Once Gideon recognized God's calling upon his life, he went into action. The Bible states that he blew a trumpet to gather the Israelite men to fight.

Nearly 32,000 men gathered around Gideon. This number probably brought comfort to Gideon's heart because the army of the enemy was large. The Bible describes it as being as thick as a swarm of locusts.

*The Compassion of Missions*

When I was working in Africa, I remember one hot season when locusts invaded one of the villages I was visiting. They were everywhere. They got into cooking pots, my suitcase and clothing, containers which stored drinking water, and everything else. It was quite an experience to find locusts sleeping in your sleeping bag with you. I think you get the message. The Midianite army was like an army of unrelenting locusts, bringing destruction across the land as it marched.

Gideon probably believed, like many others, that numbers means strength. With so many men, Gideon may have felt confident that he would certainly be able to hurt the Midianites in one way or another. But when God looked down and saw the gathering of the fighting men, He had a different thought. "Gideon, there are too many men here. When I give you victory over your enemy, it will be tempting for you to say, 'we did it in our own strength,' instead of giving me the credit and glorifying me." To make a long story short, God eventually left Gideon with only three hundred men to fight the army of the Midianites.

In 1982, two events happened in my life that reaffirmed the message that man alone is not the answer. First, I was appointed to be a missionary. I was heading to Africa. Second, I graduated from Marion College with a master's degree and high honors.

As my family and I prepared to go overseas, we had to decide what things would come with us in our suitcases and what things we would ship later. Without a second thought I knew that I wanted my framed master's degree to come in our suitcase. My wife tried to reason with me that a framed degree would add weight to our suitcase and that there was the risk of the glass shattering. But I was adamant that I wanted my degree to come with me, even if we had to pay extra for the weight at customs. It was almost as if who Jim Lo was was wrapped up in my master's degree.

As I wrapped my framed degree with layers of shirts and pants to protect it from being destroyed in transit, the following thought kept passing through my mind, "I hope the people in Africa realize how fortunate they are to get me as a missionary. I am educated. I am smart and I am talented . . . and I have a degree to prove it." (And not too bad looking either . . . only joking.)

After arriving in Zimbabwe, Roxy, the boys and I set up house in one of the suburbs of Bulawayo. One of the first things I did as we were getting our house ready for habitation was to open my suitcase, carefully take out my framed master's degree, and hang it on one of the walls of the living room. In fact, I hung it right behind the sofa. Roxy was not impressed with where I had hung it, but nothing she said would budge me to move it. I wanted everyone who visited us to see it.

> "I hope the people in Africa realize how fortunate they are to get me as a missionary. I am educated. I am smart and I am talented...and I have a degree to prove it."

I had a plan. When someone visited, I would usher them into my living room and have them sit on the sofa. I was sure that they could not miss seeing my certificate of achievement.

But things did not turn out the way that I had planned. Though we did have many individuals visiting us, none of them seemed to notice my degree. No one praised me for my learning. No one made any mention of it. I tried different strategies to get my visitors to take notice of it. Sometimes I would artificially yawn and stretch my arms wide so that one of my hands would finally end up pointing to my prized degree. But even that didn't work.

I then tried moving my degree to the entrance area of our house where it would be in the direct view of anyone who entered my house. But still the Africans who came to visit me

*The Compassion of Missions*

did not seem to see or remark about it. Since it was not getting the attention that I thought that it deserved, I finally, with great reluctance, took it down.

After twenty-some years of ministry, I have discovered that it is not the degrees on our walls that people are attracted to. In fact, no one has even asked me for my grade point average. I was wanting the people in Africa to see how important I was. I wanted them to be impressed with me. But what I am learning is that people are not so concerned with who I am and how much I know, but Who I know.

> I know Christ and I want the world to see and to know Him.
> I want them to come to Him.
> I am only a man.
> Jesus Christ is God!

## Methods alone are not the answer.

The story of Gideon also teaches us that methods alone are not the answer. The three hundred men who remained with Gideon knew how to fight. They knew different methods for fighting. They were familiar with how to use weapons of war.

*Com(e)*

But instead of giving them swords and spears, Gideon gave his men trumpets and empty jars with torches burning in them. Now what could such "foolish" weapons do to defeat an enemy that probably had iron chariots, state of the art bows and arrows, sharp swords, long spears, and bright, shiny shields for protection?

But the Israelites were not to depend on their knowledge of how to fight, or their knowledge of how to use weapons of war. They were to depend upon God.

Many in the evangelical church are familiar with the name John Maxwell. He has a powerful style of communication that God has used to touch many hearts. In the early 1990s, John came to South Africa to speak at a church growth conference. Over two thousand church leaders gathered at a large hall in Johannesburg to hear him speak. In attendance were white-Europeans, black-Africans, Indians, and even one Chinese . . . that was me. And none of us were disappointed with what we heard. Maxwell was superb. We laughed and we cried. The Lord used him in a mighty way to speak to our hearts.

**I saw white John Maxwells, black John Maxwells, and Indian John Maxwells.**

One could hear people commenting, "He is so cool!" Or "He is *lekker*."

Many who attended the conference began to think that if they would only follow Maxwell's method of preaching and teaching, they too would eventually have large, growing congregations. Everyone left the meeting pumped up to do great things.

One of my responsibilities while I was serving in Africa as a missionary was to visit our churches to encourage them and to teach church leaders. In essence, I was to bring Bible school training to pastors and lay leaders who could not leave their homes to study. In the weeks that followed the church growth conference, I began to observe that all over Southern Africa

*The Compassion of Missions*

people were imitating John Maxwell's style of preaching. I saw white John Maxwells, black John Maxwells, and Indian John Maxwells. They mimicked how Maxwell stood, how he interacted with the congregation, and even how he greeted people.

I must confess that even I tried to be like Maxwell. I tried walking and talking like him. People would hear me preach and say to me, "You've been at a Maxwell conference, haven't you?"

For months I tried to hone my John Maxwell skills. I got to the place where I could do a pretty good impersonation of John Maxwell. Then, during one of my times of communing with the Lord, He began to speak to my heart, telling me that I did not have to try to become a John Maxwell. I needed to become all that God wanted Jim Lo to be and become. I did not have to follow Maxwell's methods of preaching and ministry. Instead, I needed to seek God's direction for how I was to do ministry.

Now, do not get me wrong. John Maxwell is being mightily used by God. We can learn from him. But God doesn't need a bunch of Maxwells to do His work. He needs men and women who will individually seek Him and find His personalized will for their lives. God's work is not accomplished by following the methods of other people. It is accomplished by following the Master himself.

### Money alone is not the answer.

The story of Gideon also teaches us that money alone is not the answer. When Gideon was questioning God about why He had chosen him to lead the Israelites into battle with the Midianites, he made a very interesting statement. "My clan is the weakest in Manasseh, and I am the least in my family."

Talk about humility—Gideon had it. The word that Gideon uses which really interests me is *weakest*. Upon initially reading this passage, I thought that what Gideon was saying was that he was not very strong and muscular. I pictured Gideon being the weakling that people picked on by kicking sand onto. But even though the word *weakest* can mean this, in the Hebrew language it can also have the broader meaning of lacking in financial resources. What a wonderful revelation this was to me! Jim Lo can succeed in ministry even without a lot of monetary backing.

Now understand, I am not advocating churches to stop giving money for missions. But I am worried about the unspoken thought among many in our churches who think that money is the cure for all the problems in the world. If people are poor, give money. If people need food, give them money so they can buy some. If people need shelter, give them money so they can build.

But the reality is, money cannot take care of every problem. In fact, money which is blindly given can actually be the cause of many problems on the mission field.

> Money which is blindly given can actually be the cause of many problems on the mission field.

### Rice Christians.

The problem of interjecting money into a new field before the people are ready for it can produce "rice Christians." Perhaps some of you have never heard this phrase before. It is a phrase that has been floating around in mission circles for many years. Let me try to explain what it means.

When missionaries first entered China to spread the gospel message, they tried different ways to reach the Chinese. The missionaries thought to themselves, what can we do to get the Chinese into our churches? After many meetings they came up with a plan.

During those early years, much of China was experiencing a severe drought. Without rain the rice paddies were dust dry. Since rice is a staple in many Asian countries, the lack of rice was causing great suffering among the Chinese.

The missionaries decided to distribute free rice. They sent

*The Compassion of Missions*

letters to their home churches asking for donations. Rice was bought and sent to the missionaries, who put up signs announcing that on certain Sundays, free rice was going to be given to those who attended church.

Let me ask you a question. If you were hungry and you saw a sign announcing that you could receive free food, what would you do?

You got it. On the Sunday when the rice was to be distributed, the church was packed full. Chinese from all over wanted to get free food to feed their families. But before the rice was given to those in attendance, they were required to attend a worship service where there was singing and preaching. It was only after the service that the rice was distributed. No worship service, no rice.

The missionaries were excited about the attendance in their churches. It made them feel good to be able to report to the home church the large numbers who were claiming to be a part of their parish.

But with time the rains returned. As the rains fell, the rice paddies filled up with water. With the rice paddies full, the rice began to grow. As the supply of rice began to increase, the number of those who attended church began to dwindle.

What was the problem? There were many who professed to be Christians only because they wanted to get free rice. But with the rice problem alleviated, there was no longer any need for them to have to profess faith in Christ. They were "rice Christians."

Is the church in danger of producing rice Christians today? Allow me to share an incident from my own ministry to try to answer this question.

### "Dad, do we have to go to your church?"

It was a few days before Easter. I was pastoring a small church and like most pastors, I was hoping to have an increase in attendance on Easter Sunday morning. I was in my car, driving down Main Street, going to visit one of my parishioners. As was my custom during those early years of ministry, I had my five-year-old twin sons with me. They were seated in the back seat.

At the end of Main Street was the largest church in the community. As I slowly drove past that church, my eyes were attracted to a large banner that was hanging on the front door. On the banner were printed the words, "Come to Church on Easter Sunday! Free bunnies will be given to all the children."

I read the banner's message out loud. My voice must have been loud enough for my boys to hear, because once I uttered the last word, I felt a small hand tap me on the shoulder. I do not remember whether it was André or Matthew, but one of them asked, "Dad, do we have to go to your church? We want a bunny rabbit!"

As you may guess, this made me very sad. Not even my own children wanted to come to my church. After the visit was made, we returned home where I sat glumly in one of our living room chairs. As I sat there I came up with the following illustration that I was going to share with the members of my small congregation. Let me try to share it with you.

**Bigger and better.**

I want you to make believe that you are a board member of a church. At one of the board meetings the decision is made that the church is going to give away free bunnies. Signs are placed all over your town announcing this decision. Space in the local newspaper is bought to announce the free bunnies to the community.

Sunday morning the church is packed with people. Impatiently the children endure the preaching. You can actually hear some of them ask their parents, "Mom, when are they going to give us our rabbit?" They fidget, anticipating the moment they will be given their furry bunny.

Have you ever seen what happens with bunnies and children? I used to have a bunny rabbit when I was little. I also

*The Compassion of Missions*

had two brothers, Billy and Tommy. As children we were exposed to our share of Bugs Bunny. Bugs had long ears. Our bunny rabbit had tiny, short ears. After a brief "board meeting," my brothers and I decided that we were going to help our bunny "grow" his ears. Billy grabbed one leg, Tommy grabbed one leg, I grabbed its tiny ears, and we began to pull. That poor bunny. When we finished, it had uneven, lopsided ears. Our tortured bunny eventually died.

The children of your church come back to you and say, "Our bunny is gone. If you expect us to keep coming to your church, you must give us something bigger and better than a bunny."

The board reconvenes to discuss one issue, "What can we give that is bigger and better than a bunny rabbit?"

The board decides to give out cats. They search in barn lofts, garbage dumps, and back alleys until they obtain their quota of cats.

Sunday morning, the church is once again packed. The

sound of cat meows fills the sanctuary to the frustration of the choir members and the pastor. When the preaching is done, the children are invited to the front of the church where you, the pastor, and other leaders give each child their cat.

Have you ever seen what happens with children and cats? I have. In fact, I used to have a cat. The cat I had was a bit deformed. Instead of having a long, elegant tail, it had a bobbed tail. My friends and I did not think that it was fair for a cat to have to go through life so deformed. Thus, we had a meeting to determine how we were going to help our cat extend its tail. We came up with an ingenious idea. One person grabbed the head of the cat while I grabbed its bobbed tail and with all our strength we began to stretch it. The cat screeched and clawed. But despite our wounds, we persistently continued to stretch it until sweat dripped from the pores of our skin.

After what seemed like a long time, we decided to take a short rest to revive our strength. But once we loosened our grip on our cat, it darted away. We never saw it again.

The children again approach you and again you hear the words, "If you expect us to keep coming to your church, you will have to give us something bigger and better than a cat."

The board meets again. "What is bigger and better than a cat?"

After another long discussion, the decision is made that a dog is bigger and better than a cat. Once the meeting is adjourned, the members of the board leave the church to look for stray dogs.

On Sunday morning, the church sanctuary is filled with the sound of yelping dogs. At the end of the service, each child is given a dog.

Have you ever seen what happens with children and dogs? I have. In fact, I used to have a dog. When Roxy, André, Matthew and I first went to Africa, we inherited a dog that used to belong to the missionaries who preceded us. Sally-dog was a gentle German shepherd.

When we were first introduced to Sally-dog, we were

thrilled to have her become a part of our family. Some of our African parishioners called her Sally Lo. We wanted to be with Sally-dog all the time. We wanted her to sit near us when we ate. André, Matthew and I proposed having her take turns sleeping in bed with a different family member every night. (Roxy did not like the idea, so by a vote of one to three, Sally-dog was forced to sleep in her dog house.) We loved Sally-dog.

But do you know what happens with boys and dogs after a while? The child tends to lose interest in the dog very quickly. Before long, we boys were not feeding or watering our dog. If it weren't for Roxy, Sally-dog would have been on a forced diet.

Now let us make believe that kind-hearted Roxy was not around to feed Sally-dog. What would happen, do you think? I can tell you. Sally-dog would become despondent. Sadly, she would rest her head upon her paws and grieve over the lack of attention she was receiving. One day we would wake up and our dear Sally-dog would be nowhere to be found. She would have run away with a broken heart and an empty stomach.

The children approach the members of the church board again. By now you should already know what they are going to say. "If you want us to keep coming to church, you must give us something bigger and better than a dog." Where does it stop? I could keep going until the church had to give large elephants to the children to keep the attendance high and the attendees happy. Can you image that? Hundreds of elephants in the sanctuary! If that wouldn't mess up the carpet, I don't know what would.

**Cambodian Rice Christians.**

Some missionaries to Cambodia were being encouraged to identify some of the Cambodian Christian believers and offer them salaries to pastor churches. I was one of those missionaries. After only being in Cambodia for a very short time, word got out that I was hiring. A large number of Cambodians began to approach me and tell me why I should hire them. The only problem was that many of them were not even Christians or had been Christians for only a short period of time. With the average salary in Cambodia only twenty dollars a month and unemployment very high, one can kind of understand why many of them wanted me to hire them. I was offering them fifty dollars a month, plus extra funds for fuel and repairs to their motorbikes. After being in Cambodia for a few months, I hired our first pastor.

At first things seemed to go fairly well. Cambodians seemed to respond to the ministry of our hired pastor. It felt good to be able to report to the home church the large numbers of people who were coming to our worship services on Sunday morning. The numbers did look very good. I was receiving e-mails congratulating me for the wonderful work that I was doing.

But numbers do not tell the full story. Before long problems began to surface. I found myself having to attend meetings every week to discuss finances with those who were now a part of our church. Each week new demands were being made to me. The pastor and his wife wanted me to give them more money because they felt that what we were giving them for a salary was inadequate to meet the needs of their growing family. Two weeks after we had hired our pastor, his wife approached me and stated that since she was the "queen" of the church she also deserved a salary. At another meeting they

*The Compassion of Missions*

demanded that I buy them a new motorbike with a revved up motor. They did not feel it was fair that they had to use their own motorbike to do church business.

One Saturday the pastor and his wife informed me that they wanted to take me for a ride. Eagerly, I accepted their offer. I love visiting new places. After traveling for about thirty minutes, we entered a small village. We passed many houses that were on stilts as well as a bamboo-walled school and numerous Buddhist temples. Being in a village I had never been in before excited me. The pastor expertly swerved his motorbike around jaywalking pigs, ducks, and dogs. It was quite an adventure for me. Eventually we came to an open field next to a slow-moving river. We got off our bikes to observe the beauty of the scene before us.

As I was enjoying the view, the pastor cleared his throat and said, "We have brought you to this place because this is the land we want you to buy for us. We want to live in this village. The land will cost three thousand dollars. And once the land has been bought, we will need fifteen hundred dollars to build our house."

I was surprised at their demand. When I explained that I did not have funds to build a personal home for them, the pastor became belligerent. "You're lying to us. You have money. You're just being selfish. If you do not give us money for this land and for our house, things will not go well with you."

Sunday school teachers also began to make demands of us, telling Roxy and me that if we did not pay them a salary they would stop teaching. They did not understand why we were paying someone to be a pastor but not paying them to be teachers. The man who played the guitar during Sunday worship services also wanted a part of the financial pot. He demanded that we buy him a new guitar, a public address system and three microphones.

I started to dread Tuesday nights, for I knew that on that night a delegation from the church would be coming to my house to make their demands. Their feeling was, "Why shouldn't we make our demands? You're rich Americans. You have money!"

Eventually our ties with this pastor and congregation had to be severed. We could no longer satisfy their continually growing demands for money. They were just as willing for the separation as we were. They were now free to be able to locate other missionaries who would meet their demands for larger salaries, new motorbikes, and building funds.

### Kalenge, a committed Christian.

But again I would not want to leave you with the impression that I only have negative stories to share with you. Baba Kalenge became a Christian in his later years. Before becoming a believer, he was a drunk who would pass out from drinking African brew every Friday night. But what a conversion he had! Immediately the drinking stopped. His heart became burdened for the people who lived in a village ten kilometers from where he was living. Every day, he would either walk or ride his old worn out bicycle to Sihlengeni to share with the people there about his Savior. This was no simple task, considering the fact that Kalenge was approximately sixty years old.

> We Africans have a proverb that says, "The riches of this world are like the dew drops of the grass."

Before long some of the villagers began to respond to Kalenge's witnessing efforts. They requested him to start a church so that they could learn more of what it meant to be a Christian. Kalenge approached me for advice about building a church.

As a young missionary I allowed grandiose ideas to fill my mind. "Kalenge, it is not good for you to be living so far from the people of Sihlengeni. I will get funds for us to build you a parsonage. Once we have you settled, we can then think about building a house for God."

*The Compassion of Missions*

Before I could continue, Kalenge replied, "Umfundisi Jim, what you are saying is not good. If we are going to build a house here in Sihlengeni, God's house must be built first. I am not a Christian because I want things from you missionaries. We Africans have a proverb that says, 'The riches of this world are like the dew drops of the grass.' I am a Christian because I know Jesus Christ as my Savior. He has given me something that will last for eternity. How can I be happy when I have a house but God doesn't? We must build a house for God first."

Kalenge was not a rice Christian. There were many times that the tithes and offerings of the church were very small. Many times Kalenge received less than five dollars for the whole month. But he never complained. He shared, "I preach because I love God and not money. As a Christian I trust God to supply all that I need!"

## The power is in the Master!

When my sons André and Matthew were around six years old, they were playing with some African children. They were seated in a small circle digging holes in the lawn. I decided to eavesdrop on their conversation. Have you ever heard children arguing with one another about whose father is the biggest and the strongest?

That is what my boys were doing with their friends. I was hidden from their view but I could hear them very clearly. One of the little African boys said to my sons in a very matter of fact voice, "My dad is stronger than your dad!"

I stood silently, waiting to hear how they were going to respond to this boy's statement. I thought that I knew my boys pretty well. I automatically assumed that they would defend me by saying something like, "You're wrong! Our dad is bigger and stronger than your dad."

"Boys, don't fail me now!" I said to myself.

One of my sons finally began to speak. I thought, "Here it comes! He'll defend me now."

*Com(e)*

Then I heard him say, "You know something, you're right. Your dad is bigger and stronger than our dad." My inflated posture was quickly defeated. My boys had failed me.

This incident was a reminder to me that no matter how strong I think I am, there is always someone bigger and stronger. The spiritual truth is, <u>no matter how great we may think we are, no matter how much education we may have, no matter how talented we may be, next to God we are very finite beings.</u>

The goal of missions is not to point people to man, or methods, or money. The goal of missions is to tell others about coming to Jesus Christ. When the Israelites were faced with the problem of the Midianites, they cried to the Lord for His help. In the same way, we must remember that whatever problems or difficulties we may be confronted with, we can *com* to Christ.

### "Who will supply $500?"

We were building a church in Seam Reap, Cambodia. With two Cambodian church leaders from Phnom Phen, I took a six-hour motor boat trip up the Mekong River to see how the building project was going. Upon arriving at the site and talking to the local pastor and builder, I was informed that we were five hundred dollars short. Though there were still enough materials for the next few days, once they were gone, the builders were going to have to leave with the church building incomplete.

All day long the two church leaders who had accompanied me asked, "What are you going to do?"

Their continuous questioning added to the stress that I was already experiencing. What was I going to do? Then it dawned on me. Jim, pray!

When I was again asked what I was going to do, I gave them my answer. "We are all going to pray."

They looked at me as if I had lost my mind. Though they did not say anything, I could almost hear them asking themselves, "Did he say we are going to pray?"

*The Compassion of Missions*

"Yes, that is what I said. Let us get down on our knees and pray for God to supply us with what we need."

Reluctantly, they got on their knees and clumsily began to pray aloud with me. We prayed a long time. Once we got off our knees, I sensed an overwhelming peace come over me. I knew that God understood the problem and that He would meet it in His way. My companions were not so sure. They continued to bombard me with the question, "What are you going to do about the money?"

> **They looked at me as if I had lost my mind. Though they did not say anything, I could almost hear them asking themselves, "Did he say we are going to pray?"**

I was able to confidently answer them, "God will supply!"

Two days later we headed back to Phnom Phen. Upon arriving at the two-room apartment Roxy and I were living in, Roxy informed me, "Jim, there is an e-mail message on the computer that you may be interested in reading."

The message was from a church in Elwood, Indiana. The church had just put five hundred dollars into our mission account. They wanted it to be used for any project that we needed funds for. The message was written to us on the day that I and my two Cambodian traveling partners had prayed on our knees for God to provide. Within minutes I was on a motor bike taxi, going to the homes of the two church leaders who had come with me to Seam Reap. Bursting into their apartments, I blurted out my news, "Guess what! God has supplied our need for $500!" After I explained about the e-mail message, my companions began repeating over and over, "Praise the Lord!"

*Com(e)*

## "Who will protect?"

One of my responsibilities while I was in Southern Africa was to administer the Theological Education by Extension (TEE) program. The basic concept of TEE is to equip prospective church leaders right where they are already living and ministering instead of having them come to the Bible school for training. During my last year in Africa, I was on the road 185 days, traveling the countries of Zimbabwe, South Africa, Swaziland, and Mozambique to teach with TEE.

One week I received a phone call from one of our pastors in Vosloroos, a suburb of Johannesburg, South Africa. "Umfundisi Lo, can you come and teach at our church this weekend? Other pastors from the district will be here."

Because I am so enthusiastic about training, I quickly consented to go. What an honor to be used by God in developing men and women to minister effectively to others who are hurting and need to hear the words of eternal life.

With a bounce, I got out of bed on Saturday morning, cleaned up and got into my car to go to Vosloroos. Now you must understand something about Jim Lo. I tend to daydream once I get behind a steering wheel. I like putting Christian music tapes into my tape deck and praising my God by singing along with them. Sometimes I get into the worship so much that I begin "car seat dancing." When I get really excited, even the car "dances."

I should have noticed that something was wrong as I entered Vosloroos when I saw large rocks rolled onto the road. But, though I saw the obstructions in the road, they did not make a connection with my brain. So, I happily continued onward, singing praises at the top of my lungs.

It was the smell of burning buildings that jolted me into reality. Then I noticed that houses on both sides of the road were on fire and smoking. Large boulders blocked the entire road. I would have turned around to escape, but there was no place to make a U-turn. I could only move my car slowly toward the crowd of three hundred angry young people in the road. All of them were carrying weapons—spears, clubs, knives, and rocks.

*The Compassion of Missions*

Once I reached the crowd, the young people surrounded my car. Balling their hands into fists of fury, those closest to my car began to pound it while others began to rock it from side to side. After a few moments, which seemed like a life time, one man forcefully opened the door and commanded me to get out.

Once I was outside and vulnerable, I heard demands from different sections of the crowd. "White man (In Africa I am considered a white man. The first time I heard this I was shocked!), we want you to give us money!"

With shaking hands I took out my billfold to see how much money I had. There, looking back at me was a two rand note. At that time, two rands only converted to 75 cents. How far would 75 cents go among all these angry, demanding young people?

Then someone else shouted, "White man, give us some cigarettes!"

Now understand, I am an ordained Wesleyan preacher. I do not smoke, so I could not comply with the request.

"Let's kill the white man!"

In South Africa, a statement like that was no idle threat. Real tension existed between the white and black races. Killings were often reported in the newspapers and on television. So as you may guess, I was really scared. I began to pray and I have learned that prayers do not have to be long. My prayer that day was quite short. "Dear Lord, save me!"

As my prayer ended, someone from the back of the crowd shouted, "I've seen that guy before."

From another part of the crowd someone else yelled out, "Yeah, you're right! I've seen that guy before too!"

Then a third voice, "You know something, I've seen him before also. He's a movie star!"

Within seconds I could hear people throughout the crowd saying, "I know him too. I saw him last night at the movies. He's Bruce Lee!"

I took my hands and began to karate chop the air before me. The crowd ooohed and aaahed.

I did not ask God how to get out of my life-threatening situation. I just asked Him to save me. The African crowd was excited that Bruce Lee had visited them. To have such a well-known celebrity visit was not an everyday occurrence. (As you can guess, I did not correct their thinking). Since one does not kill a celebrity, the crowd let me go after they all touched me and I went on to teach at the church.

In a situation where I could not depend upon who I was or on methods or money, I had to depend upon God. And in a miraculous way, God delivered me, sparing my life so that I am able to recount the incident to you.

**Trust missionaries? Or trust God?**

So often we confuse those whom we have been called to minister to. We tell them that they must trust God. But unwittingly we cause them to focus their eyes on how capable we are as missionaries with our education and talents, or on the methods we employ, or on the money that we bring with us. By doing this we make it hard for them to truly see God as the answer. But missionaries, methods, and money cannot save. They may be tools that God uses to reach a lost and dying world, but it is still to Christ, the Master, that people must come.

Flora Bell Slater worked many years as a missionary in the Philippines. One day, one of the Bible school students knocked on the door of her house. "Miss Slater, I need soap to bathe. No one has sent me any. Could you please give me a bar of soap?"

But instead of giving the student some soap, Flora Bell decided that she wanted the student to learn to depend on God. She told him to go and pray for God to provide and promised him that she would also be praying for him. The next day, a package came for the young man from his home church. As he opened the box, there, sitting on top of the other items, was a bar of bathing soap. There was great rejoicing that day at the Bible school.

Flora Bell could have easily given the young student the soap he had requested. But she wanted to teach him a spiritual lesson. She wanted to point him to God and teach him to put his full trust in the Great Provider!

> **Missionaries, methods, and money cannot save. They may be tools that God uses to reach a lost and dying world, but it is still to Christ, the Master, that people must come.**

One way to test the purity of gold is to look into a bowl of the molten metal. If you can see your own face reflected clearly, all the impurities have been burned away and the gold is pure. It must be the desire of all missionaries for the people around them to see Jesus reflected in their everyday living. But as with gold, there is only one way this can happen—through the refining fire. Only when the Refiner sees His own image reflected in a heart will that image be reflected to others around. And only when needy people see Christ reflected in us will they be able to understand our message to *come to Jesus*!

# Compass

A second word that I find in the big word *compassion* is *compass*.

C-o-m-p-a-s-s-i-o-n

### My G.I. Joe compass.

When I was around ten years old, G.I. Joe was the "in" thing. All my school buddies had G.I. Joes. Not wanting to be left out of the gang, I decided that I also wanted a G.I. Joe. My brothers made fun of me for wanting to play with a doll, but my thinking was, "How could you call G.I. Joe a doll? He was strong. He was manly. He was an action-pack hero."

But along with G.I. Joe came all of the necessary accessories. There were G.I Joe caps, G.I. Joe boots, G.I. Joe clothing, G.I. Joe guns, G.I. Joe flashlights. But what I liked most was the G.I. Joe compass. I carried that compass everywhere I went. I was fascinated with how the needle always pointed north. No matter what I did to my compass, it would still point north. I would spin myself round and round with my compass in my hand, thinking that I could confuse the needle so that it would point south, or east, or west. But all I managed to do was get dizzy and frustrated, for the needle always pointed north. <u>Just as a compass always points in the same direction, so must missionaries always always point people to Christ.</u>

*The Compassion of Missions*

**Missionaries—pointing others to Christ.**

The first church my family and I visited when we arrived in Zimbabwe was out in a village. The village was inhabited by gold mine workers and their families. I was excited and wondered what a village church would be like. I knew that it was going to be very different from the churches I had attended in America, but even with this knowledge, I was not prepared for what I saw.

The village was about thirty minutes away from the city of Bulawayo. Once we got off the main blacktopped road, we had to drive our vehicles over bumpy, pot-holed, dirt paths. After having our stomachs bounced up, down, and sideways, we finally arrived at the village. A crowd of Africans was standing on the outskirts of the village. When we got out of the car, the Africans began making trilling sounds and dancing toward us. When they reached us, some in the crowd ushered us into the village. How fascinating! My first close-up exposure to Africans and an African village.

> I had been told during missionary orientation to learn to smile a lot. And that is what I did. I smiled until my smiling muscles hurt.

The smiling faces of the Africans made us feel warmly welcomed. Though we felt a bit uncomfortable because we did not fully understand what was happening, we knew that we were in safe hands. We were among Christian believers—brothers and sisters in the Lord. I felt a spiritual bond with them. Although I could not communicate with words since I did not know the Sindebele language yet, I was able to communicate nonverbally. I had been told during missionary orientation to learn to smile a lot. And that is what I did. I smiled until my smiling muscles hurt.

The church building was like no church building I had ever worshipped in. It was a simple structure. As we prepared to enter, I made some quick observations. There were no stained glass windows. In fact there were no windows at all. The walls of the church were made from 55 gallon drums that had been hammered flat. The roof was made of thatched grass.

Once my eyes finally adjusted to the dark interior, I saw that tiny holes had been punched into the flattened steel drums. These allowed light and air to enter the church. On one side of the church was an assortment of old, rickety chairs. The chair I was motioned to sit on was made of metal scraps that had been sloppily welded together.

The Africans who entered to worship with us sat on straw mats spread out upon the ground. As I sat waiting for the service to begin, I could feel the eyes of the African worshippers staring at me. While they stared, I thought to myself, "How they can worship in a place like this . . . without pews, piano, or pulpit?"

But worship they did. I was treated to singing as I had never heard singing before. It was beautiful. Though I could not understand the words being sung, I knew that they were words of praise, which were being lifted up to the Great *Unkulunkulu*.

At one point of the service, some of the older women got up from their mats and began to dance praises to the Lord. I thought that the dancing would detract from the service. But I was in for a surprise. The singing and the dancing actually enhanced worship.

After the singing and numerous specials, we were introduced to the congregation and then an African man stood up to speak. He had been chosen by the rest of the church attendees to be the spokesman. "Abafundisi, we are so glad you have come to Africa. We are glad that you have come to minister the Word of God to us. We are so thankful for you missionaries," he said through an interpreter. Then turning to the congregation, he said, "We must never forget what a

*The Compassion of Missions*

blessing it is that God has sent us missionaries. They have come here to help point us to Jesus and His Heaven."

The compass is an instrument which gives direction. Christians are to direct people to Jesus Christ, who is our compass to salvation, sanctification, and service.

## Jesus Christ, our compass to salvation.
### *"Please point me to Jesus!"*

At first, Solomon Kalenge always avoided me. When he saw me entering his village, he would get on his bike and go somewhere else. He did not want to talk to me. Though his wife and some of his children were Christians, Solomon was far away from God. He allowed those in his family who were believers to attend church, but he himself never came. I had tried to talk to Solomon about the welfare of his soul. But the one time that he was willing to talk with me, he just laughed at what I had to say.

I first met Solomon in the early 1980s when he was contemplating taking a second wife. His first wife was getting old and he wanted one who was younger, prettier, and more energetic. Talk had it that he was interested in a sixteen-year-old girl who was living in an adjacent village.

Solomon was also a heavy drinker. On Friday nights, after working hard in the gold mine, he would go to the nearby African *shebeen* (bar) and drink African home brew with his drinking buddies. With working, drinking and negotiating for his second wife, Solomon did not feel that he had time to listen to me talk about Jesus Christ. I shared with him that one can only run away from God for so long. The time would come when he would have to make a decision concerning what he would do with Christ. He again laughed at me. But that time came sooner than he had anticipated.

I was in my office at home, studying the Sindebele language, when I heard a rattle at my gate. I tried to ignore it since I did not want to be interrupted from my language study. But the rattle got louder and lasted longer. Before long I realized that whoever was making the noise was not going to go away until I went out to speak to them.

There, standing at the gate was Anna, one of Solomon's daughters. "Umfundisi, my father is at Mpilo Hospital. You must go visit him. The doctors say that he is going to die."

Though I heard her words, I did not understand her message. "What do you mean your father is dying? I just saw him the other day. He seemed pretty healthy to me, riding his bike and avoiding me." If you had been standing there, you would have heard the sarcasm in my voice.

Anna proceeded to explain in greater detail what had happened to her father. On Friday night, as was his routine, he had gone to the shebeen to drink with some of his workmates. Solomon was quite drunk when he left. Wobbling, he began the long trek to his own hut but fell down halfway back and blacked out. The next day, as the sun came over the horizon, some children who were going to the pump to fetch water found him sprawled out on the dirt path, still unconscious. Recognizing

Solomon, one of little boys ran to the village to get help. Solomon was then taken to the hospital. When the doctors examined him, they discovered that he was not able to see. They concluded that he must have drunk contaminated home brew. Their diagnosis was that he did not have very long to live.

Anna finished by saying, "Umfundisi, you must go and speak to my father. You must go and tell him about Jesus Christ and point him to the way of salvation."

> "My father is dying and you won't even go talk to him. How can you call yourself a missionary?"

"Anna, I don't think I can do that. I have tried many times to tell him about Jesus Christ and how he can be saved. But your father has avoided me. Why should I keep wasting my time? He'll just ignore me and my words again. If he dies without Christ, it is not my fault. It is his own fault. I gave him plenty of opportunities to listen and respond."

Anna looked at me, tears rolling down her face. "And you call yourself a missionary. Your job is to point people to Jesus. My father is dying and you won't even go talk to him. How can you call yourself a missionary?"

If any one tells you that using guilt to get something accomplished does not work, they are fooling you. Anna's words made me feel small and guilty. After apologizing to her for my wrong attitude, we got into my car and drove to the hospital.

African hospitals seldom have private rooms. Patients are placed in large wards with around fifty others. Mpilo Hospital was like this. We climbed the stairs to the third floor where the men's ward was. I entered the nurses' area to see if they could tell me anything new about Solomon. The head nurse looked at her charts and stated that there was no

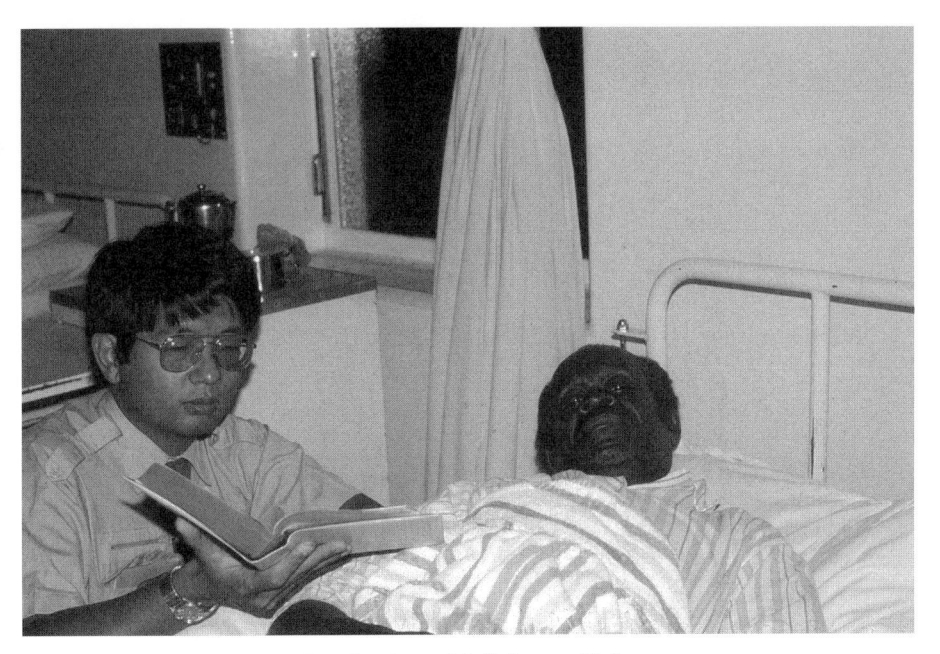

*Jim Lo sharing with Solomon Kalenge*

change. Solomon was still blind, very weak, and the doctors were not giving him a good chance of surviving. All through this conversation, Anna leaned silently against the door frame of the office. She was finding it hard to believe that her father could die.

I asked the nurse to direct me to where Solomon was and I then turned to Anna.

"Anna, listen. I will talk to your father about Jesus Christ, but you must help me. Since my Sindebele is not very good, I will need you to translate for me."

Anna and I reached Solomon's bed and looked down on a face that seemed to have grown twenty years older since I had seen him just a few days before. Solomon's breathing was shallow and labored.

"Baba Kalenge, this is Umfundisi Lo. I am here with your daughter Anna. We have spoken to the nurses and they tell us that you are very sick. Anna wanted me to come and speak to you about Jesus Christ and about how you can go to heaven. Do you mind if I share with you?"

*The Compassion of Missions*

He gave no response. I took this to mean that I could proceed to share with him. For the next thirty minutes I tried to point him to Jesus Christ. I recited different passages of Scripture to him.

"Baba Kalenge, the Bible tells us that all have sinned and fallen short of the glory of God. That includes me and it includes you. Sin prevents us from entering into heaven because God is a holy God. Because He is holy, He cannot have sin near Him. Does this make sense to you?"

Again I took Solomon's silence to mean yes.

"One of my favorite verses in the Bible is John 3:16. It says, 'For God so loved the world, that he gave his one and only Son, that whoever believes in him shall not perish but have eternal life.' Baba Kalenge, would you like eternal life?"

Again I was met with silence. But since he raised no objections or questions, I proceeded to talk, thinking to myself, "Boy, Jim, this has to be one of the most unresponsive soul-winning appointments you have ever had."

I explained to Solomon how a person could be saved. First, I spoke to him about needing to repent (ukupenduka) from his sins. Second, I wanted him to know that I had no power to save him since I was just a human being like he was. I wanted him to understand that he had to believe (ukukholwa) and trust (ukuthemba) Jesus Christ for his salvation. Third, I explained that he had to confess (ukuvuma) his sins to God and then receive (ukwamukela) Christ into his life.

When I finished going through the plan, I was not sure what to do next. Should I ask him if he wanted to become a Christian or not? I hesitated a long time.

Anna finally asked me, "Umfundisi, aren't you going to ask my father if he wants to be a Christian?"

It was only because of Anna's prodding that I asked, "Baba Kalenge, what would you like to do with what I have just shared with you?"

Slowly, Kalenge reached over and pulled back the bed sheet that was covering him. He then sat up, swung his legs over the side of the hospital bed, and then gingerly placed his feet on the hard, tiled floor. Because of his blindness, Solomon could not see where I was standing, but he followed my voice. When he sensed that he was close to me, he knelt down upon the floor, wrapped his arms around my legs and cried out,

"Umfundisi Lo, I want to be a Christian. Please point me to Jesus."

The other men in the ward were watching us and I felt a bit embarrassed. On the other hand, Kalenge had only one thing on his mind. He wanted to become a Christian. He was not concerned with who was looking at him.

Self-consciously I knelt next to him and led him through the sinner's prayer. With tears flowing from his sightless eyes and down his weary face, Solomon became a child of the King.

### *"Who is that man?"*

When I was in Cambodia, I heard an interesting story about a little girl named Khom Tot. In 1975, Khom Tot lived with her family in a village near the Thailand border. Khom Tot spent her time playing with the other children of the village and life was peaceful.

But one day the leaders of Khom Tot's village heard that the Khmer Rouge army was approaching. The Khmer Rouge was a communist guerrilla group that took over the country that year. They stole food from the people, burned houses down, and killed thousands of people.

The people of the village were terrified. What could they do? All options risked death. Some decided that they would stay. Others decided that they would try to walk to Thailand where it was much safer.

Khom Tot's father and mother hesitated. The journey would be a dangerous one. It would mean walking over forty miles through thick jungles filled with long, sharp thorns that could go right through a person's foot, wild animals, and patrolling Khmer Rouge soldiers. But Khom Tot's parents decided that they should still try to escape from Cambodia.

*The Compassion of Missions*

Around seventy other villagers also decided to try to make the journey to Thailand. So on a moonless night, the group began their long walk. Everyone was told that they had to keep very quiet. If the Khmer Rouge soldiers spotted them, the soldiers would execute them all.

Khom Tot clung to her mother's hand. When she got too tired to walk, her father carried her. They walked for hours in the dark jungle. Mosquitoes bit them viciously. Sometimes they would see snakes slithering away and hear the growling of wild cats. During the day, they continued to walk in the hot rays of the sun. Sweat streamed down their bodies.

After three days of walking, everybody was exhausted and some were getting discouraged. The food they had carried along with them was running out. There was very little drinking water left. Their cloth shoes were worn out from the sharp rocks and thorns.

By the fourth night, many of the weary travelers were ready to give up and try to return to their village. They decided to stop for a rest and discuss what they should do. As they were sitting, Khom Tot noticed some fireflies beginning to gather at a certain spot. Before long, hundreds of fireflies filled the air with a strange glow. All the villagers turned to stare at the light and saw a man standing in the middle of the fireflies. With a voice that brought courage to the group, he said, "Come and follow me. I will lead you to safety in Thailand."

The group got up one by one from where they were sitting and began to follow the man with the glowing fireflies flying around him. They could hear the voices of Khmer Rouge soldiers nearby, but they were able to continue walking without being detected. After walking for a few hours, the man turned and said to them, "You are now in Thailand!"

The villagers hugged each other in relief and happiness. When they turned to thank the man, he was gone. Someone asked, "Who was that man?" Everyone was silent because no one knew.

In Thailand the villagers settled into a camp with other Cambodian refugees. One day as Khom Tot was exploring the camp, she noticed a large building. Curious, she tip-toed to the door and peeked in. She saw many people kneeling on the floor. They seemed to be talking to someone, but not to each other. Her eyes explored the inside of the building, stopping at a picture on the front wall. Khom Tot's eyes grew large. She ran into the room, pointed to the picture and asked, "Who is that man?"

One of the ladies came to Khom Tot and said, "Why, that is Jesus Christ, the Son of God." Then the lady asked Khom Tot, "Would you like to know more about Him?"

Khom Tot answered, "I know Him already. He is the man who led us out of Cambodia."

Tears began to roll down the cheeks of the lady. "You are an answer to prayer," she said. "We are Christians. Every day we gather in this church to ask God to help Cambodians reach this refugee camp safely. We pray this way because we want

*The Compassion of Missions*

to tell them about how God can forgive their sins. We want to tell them how they can go to heaven."

Khom Tot said, "If Jesus was able to lead us safely out of Cambodia, I know that He can lead me safely to heaven." That day Khom Tot became a Christian.

### Jesus, our compass to sanctification.
#### Direction through the Bible.

When coming to Jesus Christ, a person must be willing to submit to His leading. In other words, we look to Christ to direct us into His sanctification, where we surrender everything to Him and live lives that are pleasing and obedient to Him.

Since Christ directs us through the Bible, it must be the foundation of all our attitudes and actions, no matter what our culture. Now there are many things in different cultures that do not contradict what the Bible says. For example, nowhere in the Bible does it tell us what color shoes we should wear in church. For this reason, it is neither right nor wrong for a person to wear black shoes, or brown shoes, or even white shoes. In fact, in Cambodia, shoes are not worn in church at all. As people enter into the worship area, all shoes are to be left at the door. The removal of shoes in the Cambodian culture is a sign of respect. I found myself being doubly careful to make sure that my socks matched and had no holes for my toes or my heels to stick out.

But when culture counters what the Bible states, it is the Bible that must always be followed. A young girl in one of the African villages where we ministered became pregnant out of wedlock. Her parents were seen by the community as leaders in the church. Their daughter was active in Sunday school, sang specials during worship services and participated in the

> **When culture counters what the Bible states, it is the Bible that must always be followed.**

62

youth group. I decided that I needed to talk to the parents and the young pregnant girl about the situation.

As we began to talk, I sensed that there was no shame or remorse concerning the pregnancy. I was a bit surprised. In fact, the parents seemed happy about the situation. They were proud that their daughter was able to become pregnant. It took me off guard. After a few hours of frustrating talk, I finally blurted out, "Haven't you read the Bible where it talks about God looking down on sex before marriage?"

The parents replied, "What are you all worked up about? It's culturally alright for our daughter to become pregnant before marriage. Also, we don't view the Bible the same way that you do. It is a good book, but we don't believe that it is the full Word of God.

"To be truthful, our daughter getting pregnant is a blessing. It shows the eligible men in the community that she is able to bear children. They will now come seeking her to be their wife."

An African pastor was caught in adultery. The leaders of the church had to decide whether he should be disciplined. One church leader felt strongly that the pastor should not be disciplined. She reasoned, "He's an African. Culturally, it is not considered a big deal if African men fool around a little."

A visitor from the church in the Philippines came to speak to our church leaders in Africa about church planting and tithing. After he finished speaking at one service, a woman came up to him and began to scold him. She said that he had no right to preach about giving, since this only made the Africans feel guilty. Africans were too poor to give, she claimed. And it was not culturally proper for Africans to have to give in church either.

Please allow me to interject a few of my personal thoughts about giving here. <u>Giving does not depend on how much a person has. It is an attitude of the heart.</u> While working in Southern Africa, I ministered to the rich as well as to the poor. And I have observed that those who were poorer tended to be the greater givers. This seems to also be true in America. A

*The Compassion of Missions*

survey conducted in the 1980s revealed that those who gave the most to charity earned the least.

Jesus calls us to be faithful to His Word, even when it goes against our culture. And while following His direction may be hard, as in the examples above, He will be faithful to us when we obey Him.

*Annie Makusha*

Annie Makusha knitted sweaters. She would knit several at a time, and then go door to door, trying to sell them. But for weeks no one bought any of her sweaters. She became frustrated. On Sunday morning at church, as the offering basket was being passed, Annie began to come up with reasons why she could not give. But then she sensed someone speaking to her. "Annie, believers need to obey My Word. And if you will obey, I promise to bless you! Reluctantly, she gave her tithe.

The next week she again went door to door trying to sell some of her sweaters. At the first house she asked, "Would you like to buy a sweater?"

"Would I like to buy a sweater? I sure would! My child

needs one for school. Do you have a brown one?"

At the second house she again asked the question, "Would you like to buy a sweater?"

"Yes, I would. The weather has been a little chilly lately. I would like to have a warm one to wear."

At the third house she asked, "Would you like to buy a sweater?"

"I am so glad you came by today. I need to buy a gift for someone. A sweater will make a wonderful gift."

By the end of the week, Annie had sold all the sweaters she had knitted. You talk about an excited Christian. On Sunday morning she stood up in church and testified, "I am learning that when we obey God and His Word, He *will* bless us!"

### *Direction through the Holy Spirit.*

Elias Moyo had come from Victoria Falls to attend district conference in Bulawayo, Zimbabwe. Moyo looked forward to these annual conferences because they gave him opportunity to fellowship with pastors that he had not seen during the year and to find nourishment for his soul.

Elias Moyo had been serving the Lord for many years. He was the pastor at Bethesda Mission as well as Simakade. Every Sunday he would preach at the mission and then walk over six miles to preach at Simakade. This would be physically taxing for young pastors and Moyo was over seventy years old. But the joy of ministry was no longer in his heart. It had become an unpleasant chore for him. His love for his flock had turned cold. During the conference, Moyo shared with different ones that if he did not receive spiritual help, he was going to stop preaching. He needed revival.

The district conference ended with a worship service on Sunday morning. I had been asked to preach. As I stood up to share with the congregation, I silently asked the Lord to speak through me. For forty minutes I encouraged those who were listening to me to surrender their lives and enter into the experience of entire sanctification. As I began to draw my message to a close, Reverend Moyo stood up, and with tears running down his face, began to sing the words, "Thela, uMoyo oNgcwele" (pour down upon us, Holy Spirit).

Over and over he repeated these words. Then, with a glow and a smile upon his face, Moyo began to testify. "After all these years, I can now say that I have been filled with the Holy Spirit. I have a peace in my heart that I have never had before. I am totally His!"

Reverend Moyo returned to Victoria Falls a spiritually new person. People who attended the church he pastored shared with me that it seemed as if Moyo was a young man again. He had more energy than they had ever seen him have before. "Umfundisi Jim, where did he get all that energy from? And where did he get so much love for us? He preaches better than we have heard him preach in years. We like what has happened to him, but we don't understand how it happened. What did you do to him at that district conference?"

I didn't do anything. It was God. God found a person who was willing to surrender all to Him. The Holy Spirit was allowed to come and fill Moyo's heart. Moyo was sanctified by the Spirit.

### Jesus, our compass to service.

One day, while I was in my office, still studying the Sindebele language, I heard a rattle at the gate. When I went to find out who was there, I was in for a surprise. There stood Solomon Kalenge. Without thinking I blurted out, "Baba Kalenge, what are you doing here? You were supposed to die." How do you like that for tact?

According to Solomon, after I left him at the hospital, he began to spend hours praying to God. What else could he do? He could not see and he was too weak to get up to do anything. So he spent hours communing with God. In his prayers he began asking God to heal his body.

One morning when he woke up, he realized that he could see. In fact, he felt stronger than he had felt in years. At first he thought he was dreaming. But as the male ward came to life, with all its noise and activity, Solomon knew that he was awake and that God had done a wonderful thing for him.

The doctors and nurses came to Solomon's bed, expecting to find him as he had been, weak and blind. But instead they found a man who was spiritually and physically energized. Solomon could not contain the joy that was in his heart. He told me, "I could tell that the doctors and nurses were surprised and wanted answers. So, I began to preach to them. I wanted them to know that I was a Christian and God had healed me." Solomon had come by my house to thank me for leading him to Christ.

A few weeks later I again heard a rattle at my gate. "Oh, who can it be this time?"

Grudgingly, I left my language study to see who was at the gate. There stood Baba Kalenge again. After inviting him into my house, I asked, "Baba Kalenge, what can I do for you this time?" Do you sense a little bit of my irritation?

"Umfundisi Jim, I feel the Lord wants me to be a preacher!"

"What did you say? Did I hear you right? Did you say you feel that the Lord wants you to be a preacher?"

"Yebo, Umfundisi."

"Solomon, you can't be a preacher. You have never been trained to be a preacher. In fact, don't you only have a second grade education? You must have heard the Lord wrong. Go home and give up this crazy idea."

> "I could tell that the doctors and nurses were surprised and wanted answers. So, I began to preach to them. I wanted them to know that I was a Christian and God had healed me."

*The Compassion of Missions*

Dejected, Baba Kalenge left my house. I thought I had taken care of the problem.

Two weeks later I heard the rattle of my gate and once again, there stood Baba Kalenge, wanting to talk with me. "Umfundisi, I heard what you told me last time but I still feel God calling me to preach. That feeling just will not go away. In fact, the feeling seems to get stronger and stronger all the time."

"Solomon, I'll say it one more time. You cannot be a pastor. You do not have a good education. How could you train to be a pastor when you cannot even read? Go home and give up this crazy idea."

Baba Kalenge left my house with an expressionless face. He was in deep thought.

Guess who was rattling my gate again a few days later? "Baba Kalenge, what is it now?"

"Umfundisi Lo, I still feel that God wants me to be a preacher. In fact, I have been going to the village next to mine and sharing with people about Jesus Christ and what He has done for me. I have been telling the people about you and I told them I would ask you to come and preach to them."

By now I was fuming. "Solomon, are you hard of hearing? Didn't I tell you that you could not be a preacher? You should give up this crazy idea of yours to be a preacher."

But this time Kalenge was not willing to give up the fight. "Umfundisi Lo, are you greater than God?"

"What do you mean?"

"If God has called me to preach, who are you to tell me that I cannot?"

I felt that the wind had been punched out of me. I knew that Solomon had a point, but I still was not willing to give in. "Listen, Solomon. I will make you a deal. I will go and preach to those people whom you have spoken to at Sihlengeni. If there are fewer than a handful of people there, will you give up this idea of wanting to be a pastor?"

"Yebo, Umfundisi."

On Friday night I drove to where Solomon lived to pick

him up. We then drove to Sihlengeni. When we arrived in the village, the sun had already gone behind the horizon. I parked my vehicle on the side of the dirt road and Solomon and I began walking the cattle trails to reach a distant hut. Though there was a chill to the night, I was beginning to sweat from the exertion of walking.

When we arrived at our destination, Solomon motioned for me to allow him to go in first. In obedience, I followed him in. It was dark inside the hut. A few candles gave a meager amount of light. At first, I could only make out a few faces. I thought, "This should show Kalenge that he is not preacher material."

But as my eyes adjusted to the darkness, I was surprised by the number of people who had gathered. On the round floor of the hut sat over thirty-five Africans. They had come to listen to Baba Kalenge's "umfundisi" share the Word of God with them. It was a wonderful night. For hours they sat listening to me share about Jesus Christ and His love. At the end of my sharing, I asked if any of them would like to receive Jesus Christ as their personal Savior. One brave soul raised her hand and said, ". . . but Umfundisi, we already know Jesus Christ as our Savior. Baba Kalenge prayed with us to become Christians a few days ago. We were wondering if you would help us start a church here. And we were wondering if Baba Kalenge could be our pastor."

As I sat there in the hut, surrounded by pleading African believers, I realized that Kalenge was right. God had called him to preach and serve the villagers of Sihlengeni. Who was I to stand in his way? Kalenge had to follow the guidance of the Great Compass, Jesus Christ.

Since that night Solomon has become a wonderful pastor. He spends hours serving others in the village. If there is a death, he is the first one to help dig the grave. If someone needs help to plow a field, or raise the roof of a hut, or plaster the sides of a school building, or dig a hole for an outhouse, Solomon is there to help.

Within a short period of time, over seventy individuals were coming to hear Solomon preach the Word of God.

One day, while I was visiting the village, I asked some of the men why they attended Solomon's church. One older man replied, "Kalenge is the worst preacher I have heard. But I come to this church because I know that God has done something special for Kalenge. He has changed. He was once a drunk, and now he is always sober. He used to hate his wife, but now he loves his wife. He used to beat his children unjustly, but now he treats them with great kindness. We come to his church because we know that he knows God and God knows him!"

# Passion

A third word that I see in the big word *compassion* is *passion*.

### C-o-m-**p-a-s-s-i-o-n**

Passion is synonymous with *fervor, enthusiasm, zeal,* and *urgency.* It also carries the idea of *ardor,* meaning to burn.

Charles Wesley, the famous revivalist and hymn writer, was asked one time, "Why is it that people are so drawn to you . . . just like a magnet?"

Wesley replied, "Well, you see, when you set yourself on fire, people love to come and watch you burn!" Wesley understood about passion.

Those involved in missions must have passion. In Romans 10:13-14, we have what is called the Christian Mandate.

> *Everyone who calls on the name of the Lord will be saved.*
> *How, then, can they call on the one they have not believed in?*
> *And how can they believe in the one of whom they have not heard?*
> *And how can they hear without someone preaching to them?*

*The Compassion of Missions*

I can almost see Paul writing these words. It is late at night. He could not sleep because he is burdened for those who are around him and are spiritually lost. His heart burns for the salvation of lost souls. But Paul does not write as one who feels defeated by the weight of the burden. Instead, he has a passionate vision. His vision is for this world to be under the lordship of Jesus Christ.

As I read the Gospels, I see a small group of men who were captured by the same passionate vision. I see in the book of Acts believers who were also enveloped by this vision . . . a vision that the kingdom of God could be brought here, on earth . . . a vision that burned deep within their hearts. It was this passionate vision that drove them to

*pray,*
*go,*
*and give.*

### A passion to pray.

The church of Jesus Christ needs believers who have a passion that drives them to their knees. While I was ministering in Mozambique, I had opportunity to converse with many Africans about the welfare of their souls. Once one African said, "You Christians talk about passion for God, but it is all talk."

I did not like what he was saying. I demanded that he give me an example to prove his point. Without hesitation he answered, "Prayer."

I had to admit to myself that there was truth in what he had answered. Muslims around the world put many Christians to shame with their fervency for prayer. How many of us faithfully pray three times a day?

I was exposed to Islamic fervency for prayer while I was in Mozambique. Early in the morning, even before the sun had awakened, I would hear the Muslim cry over public address systems hung all around the city, calling them to prayer. It was quite a convicting sight to watch them spread out their mats upon the ground, get on their knees, and in unison begin to recite their prayers.

Fervency for prayer can also be seen among the Buddhists. They will stand before a statue of Buddha, praying to him for hours on end. In one area of southeast Asia, Buddhist monks are given the opportunity to enter into an intensive prayer retreat. The commitment they make is not to just pray for a few minutes or even for a few hours. The prayer retreat lasts for three years, three months, three days, and three hours. During this period they live and pray in a tiny, dark, mountain grotto. They exist on bread and water fed to them once a day. When the three years, three months, three days and three hours come to an end, they are asked if they would like to recommit themselves to another three years, three months, three days and three hours of prayer. In many cases the answer is "yes." I was speechless when I heard this.

> "Solomon, I could give you my answer. But what you really need is God's answer."

Such commitment to prayer is rooted in passion. After pastoring the church in Sihlengeni for around two years, Solomon Kalenge realized that it was not growing as quickly as it had been growing at first. Concerned, he came to visit me. "Umfundisi Jim, something is wrong. People don't seem to be responding to our witness any more. What can we do to change this?"

"Solomon, I could give you my answer. But what you really need is God's answer. Take some time and ask the Lord to show you what He would want you to do."

A few days later I made a trip to visit Solomon at his home. As we fellowshipped over strong, hot tea, I asked him whether or not God had revealed to him what he should do. Taking his Bible, Solomon opened it and began turning its pages. "Umfundisi, I want to read you some verses that I believe God has directed me

*The Compassion of Missions*

to. Jesus said, 'The harvest is plentiful but the workers are few. Ask the Lord of the harvest, therefore, to send workers into his harvest fields.' Umfundisi, the answer is God wants me to pray! He wants me to pray for souls and for workers."

Having found God's answer, Solomon began to pray as he had never prayed before. He would wake up early in the morning, before anyone else in his family, and spend many hours communing with God and asking Him for workers. Solomon also asked God to speak to his neighbors who did not know Jesus Christ as their Savior.

Many times he would skip meals to fast and pray for the lost. Every night he would call his entire family together for a time of prayer, where names of lost people were presented and prayers for workers to enter into the harvest fields were again lifted up to the Lord.

Did Solomon enjoy praying at first? Was praying fun for him? The answer to both questions is "no."

Solomon shared, "It was an ordeal for me to pray. I did not like to get up early. But as I continued to discipline myself in this area of my spiritual life, prayer began to become a habit. It got to the point that if I did not pray, I did not feel good about myself. In fact, I began to recognize that if I had not prayed my day did not go well. After many months, prayer has become a way of life for me. I would feel lost and empty if I did not spend time every day in sweet fellowship with my God."

Did God answer Solomon's prayers? The answer is "yes," and in a mighty way.

Almost a year after coming to talk to me, Solomon asked me to participate in a baptismal service that he was conducting at the Sihlengeni Wesleyan Church. During the year thirty villagers had surrendered their lives to Christ. They were now wanting to publicly give testimony to others in the village that they were Christians.

Numbered in this group of baptismal candidates were two young men, Sikhumbuzo Ndlovu and Elmon Dlodlo. Faithfully, they had attended the new converts' Bible study classes that Baba Kalenge taught every week. They also attended Sunday school and Sunday church services. When they found out that Kalenge was having early prayer meetings, they also began to attend those. And when they found out that he was having evening prayer meetings, they began to attend those as well.

It seemed that the more Sikhumbuzo and Elmon prayed, the more they wanted to please and do things for God. One day they approached Baba Kalenge and shared that they felt that God was wanting them to go evangelizing with him. Thus, a "witnessing team" of three was formed. Wherever Baba Kalenge went, Sikhumbuzo and Elmon also went. Baba Kalenge would talk to the older villagers. Sikhumbuzo and Elmon would speak to the younger ones.

Many young people began to commit their lives to Christ. To help them grow spiritually and be encouraged by other Christians their age, Sikhumbuzo and Elmon started a youth group. There were times when over thirty young people would gather to learn about God and sing songs of praise to Him.

During one of the Sunday worship services in which I had been invited to speak, I preached about God's call to

*The Compassion of Missions*

full-time ministry. During the time of invitation, I asked those who were sensing God calling them into His service to come forward.

Not many responded. Perhaps the reason for the low response was because of what I had shared. There were some in the congregation who had been spreading the word around that if they became preachers, missionaries would provide them with a monthly salary and ministry allowance. I wanted to squelch that rumor right away. Therefore, I told those in the congregation that there were no guaranteed salaries from America for those who wanted to be pastors. It was the responsibility of national believers to take care of their own pastors. I also stressed the point that often, *abafundisi* had to live by faith, depending upon God for their food, clothing, and housing since giving in African churches was typically so low.

As the invitational song was being song, two individuals walked forward. You guessed right. It was Sikhumbuzo and Elmon.

As they stood there in front of the entire congregation, I reviewed the main points of my message. "Sikhumbuzo and Elmon, as you stand here, I want to make sure that you understand fully what you are commiting to. You are testifying to the believers of this church that you sense God calling you into full-time ministry. It is not the Wesleyan denomination that is calling you . . . or even a missionary that is calling you. It is God who does the calling.

I also want you to understand that it may not always be easy for you to be pastors. . . . You are going to have to trust God to take care of you . . . and this includes financially. That will take great faith."

As I began to come to the end of my discourse, Sikhumbuzo spoke up. "Umfundisi Lo, we understand all that you have said. Elmon and I are answers to Baba Kalenge's prayers for workers to work in the harvest fields. We do not stand up here because we want salaries from missionaries. We are standing here because we know God has called us to serve him with our whole lives. Because God has called us, we know that He will also take care of us."

Solomon's passion for God drove him to his knees. For months he faithfully prayed. God rewarded him for his efforts. Many villagers living in Sihlengeni have surrendered their lives to Christ. Sikhumbuzo is presently pastoring a church in Victoria Falls and Elmon is pastoring a church in the Bulawayo township of Entumbani. God does answer our passionate prayers for the lost and for workers.

> "Because God has called us, we know that He will also care for us."

## A passion to go.

When I was a little boy, my brother and I found a box of matches. We went to our bedroom and closed the door for secrecy. Sitting on my bed, we began to "produce" fire. However, in our excitement we got careless. One of the burning matches fell onto the bed. Within seconds the wool blanket on top of the mattress caught on fire, and the fire began to spread.

Tommy quickly moved into action. He ran towards the bathroom to get water to douse the flames. However, when he realized that I was not following him, he turned around to see what I was doing. I was sitting there, petrified by terror. Tommy yelled, "Jim, why are you just sitting there? We've got a fire to put out!" His voice of alarm moved me to action.

People without Christ are heading for eternal punishment. For this reason believers can not afford to be apathetic to the present spiritual condition of the world. We need to move into action. We need a passion that moves us to go!

Over the years I have had the wonderful opportunity to work with many missionaries. You may know some of them. Bob and Eva Cheney, Orai and Linda Lehman, Jim and Carol

Ramsay, and Don and Elizabeth Karns are a few who immediately come to my mind. Though each one of them came from different backgrounds and have different personalities and spiritual gifts, they all had a passion which energized them to leave the comforts of their homes, families and friends to go and preach the Good News to people of a different culture.

Richard Nukery is a dear friend of mine. He is an African, belonging to the Shaangaan tribe. At one Southern African Regional Conference, Richard, with hundreds of others, heard the pleas of an old retired minister, asking for someone young and energetic to go and minister in Venda, in the northern part of South Africa. Though Richard heard the plea, it basically went in one ear and out the other. He was already involved in ministry. Why would he want to uproot himself and go to a tribe that was different from his own?

But the Lord began to speak to his heart. He began to lay a burden on Richard's heart for the those living in Venda. Before long Richard's entire life was preoccupied with the desire to minister in Venda. After much prayer, he and his wife Rose packed their belongings and went. They left friends and family in obedience to God's call. They were filled with a passion to please their God . . . a passion which moved them to go.

Jun and Mamel Raphael are Filipinos. While in the Philippines, the Raphaels pastored a church that was experiencing wonderful numerical growth. They were happy and comfortable. What else could they want? The church was healthy. The congregation loved them. Jun was being groomed for leadership roles in the district. Someone told me, "They are rising stars."

But during a missions convention, Jun and Mamel were filled with a passion to go and minister to those living in Cambodia. In 1992, it was reported that less than 1% of the Cambodian population knew Jesus Christ as their Savior. While this statistic discouraged others, it energized Jun and Mamel. They saw it as a challenge. And challenges are God's opportunity to do miracles. Those in their church tried to talk them out of leaving. But their desire to preach the gospel to Cambodians kept growing.

In 1996, the Rafaels left the familiarities of the Philippines and arrived in Cambodia for their first term of missionary service. I can remembering sitting with Jun and Mamel, counseling them when waves of homesickness and loneliness swept over them. But never did I hear them want to give into those feelings to return home. Passion had moved them to go and passion was holding them steady.

<u>Passion moves people to go beyond their comfort zones</u>. I was with ten of my students in Cambodia on a short term mission trip. We were visiting Buding to encourage Cambodians who had just recently become Christians. As we entered the small room where we were gathering for worship, we were ambushed by an army of flies.

The flies were horrible. Hundreds of them crawled all over the exposed parts of our bodies, irritatingly tickling our faces, arms, and hands. Some of them sought to enter our noses and ears, while others journeyed up our arms and legs. I feared smiling lest those pesky, flying insects would take a nose dive into my mouth. My students and I tried every means we could think of to keep those flies off of us. Some of my students waved their arms. A few of them tried blowing them away. I wagged my head from side to side. Though all this would give us a few seconds of relief, the flies would eventually land back on our faces and bodies, resuming their torment.

There is no trash pickup at Buding. For more than twenty years, the garbage of people living in squatter conditions has been carelessly thrown outside their homes, forming large piles. Every inch of ground was covered with kitchen scraps, old newspapers, discarded clothing, and human waste. The sour, fermented smell that accompanied the rotting garbage was almost unbearable.

After the long worship service, we all headed back to Jun and Mamel's home. While my students were beginning to

*The Compassion of Missions*

*Street in Buding*

wind down, I drew Jun aside and said, "Jun, can we go someplace where we can talk in private?"

Upon entering the privacy of Jun's office, I firmly stated, "Jun, I do not want to go back to Buding again. Couldn't you have started a church in a better location? It was horrible there. Those flies crawling on me made me feel dirty all over."

After a few seconds of silence, Jun gently replied, "Jim, I am so sorry you feel the way that you do."

He then asked me a question, "Have you seen paintings of the crucified Christ?"

I nodded that I had.

Jun continued, "I have too. But I do not think that any one of them adequately depicts the horrors of that event. For one

*Passion*

thing, the paintings that I have seen do not show the flies that harassed Jesus Christ as He hung upon that cross. It just makes sense to me that there would have been flies there. After being so cruelly scourged, there had to have been blood dripping from the wounds caused by the tentacles of the Roman soldier's whip. There was plenty of blood to attract flies to his body.

"I am sure that Jesus wanted to 'shoo' those flies away. But He was a prisoner trapped on the cross, His arms rendered immovable by the spikes. And yet, the reality is that it was not the spikes that kept Jesus upon that cross. It was His passionate love for mankind. Christ endured the torments of the flies because He loved us."

Looking straight into my eyes, Jun then asked me, "Jim, is it too much for us to endure the torments of some flies to be able to minister to individuals who need God's love? Shouldn't our hearts so overflow with the passionate love of God that we are willing to minister to others even when it is not fun or comfortable."

Jun was right. Ministry will not always be easy. But this should not deter us from doing ministry. <u>Our passionate love for God and for our neighbor must be our motivating factor for ministry . . . not whether it will be easy or difficult.</u>

### A passion to give.

What would you do if you were given $10,000? Jerry and Darlene had received $10,000 and were praying about what the Lord would want them to do with it. A few weeks later, they heard about a particular ministry that was in need of financial assistance. It was a ministry that was reaching many with the message of God's love. After hearing the plea for help, they wrote out a check for $10,000 without hesitation. Did they later regret their decision to give? Jerry, in his usual jovial style of speech shared, "Jim, can one ever outgive God?" Passion to reach the world with the gospel message moved Jerry and Darlene to give.

*The Compassion of Missions*

### *The flashlight.*

All week long we had been receiving mail asking for some type of donation. Charity organizations sent pictures of poor people to work on our emotions. Colleges asked that we give out of loyalty. Different Christian groups stressed that Christians needed to be supporting other Christians. And then on Sunday, the pastor preached on giving to finance the work of the church. As I drove home, I began to rebel in my heart against everything I had heard and read for the past week that dealt with giving.

"Lord, I'm willing to give my tithe, but anything above that just isn't fair. Besides, my salary isn't that great. I can't just give to everybody who asks me. I have a family to support."

A week later I was in Mozambique. The night was dark and humid and the crickets were playing their mournful songs. I was walking with twelve African Christian brothers and sisters. It was hard walking because of the deep sand. Every once in a while I found myself stumbling forward, but was steadied by those walking by my side. My eyes were not accustomed to the darkness. My legs were not used to the quick pace of my African friends. Sweat dripped down my face. My shirt was saturated. We were going to church.

I began to think I was doomed to die—drowned in my own sweat—when we finally arrived at our destination. Many people had already gathered to hear the foreign missionary preach God's Word. A wooden table was placed under a dim light bulb which was hung from the branch of an old weathered tree. Children sat on the bare ground. Women sat on straw mats. The men sat on long benches. The blackness of the night served as the walls of the church.

For an hour people stood up, gave testimonies, sang specials, and thanked me for coming to visit them. The time for receiving the offering was then announced. People began to locate their money. Men dug deep into their pockets. Women took out knotted hankies and untied them so that they could count the precious coins that they were going to give. Children relaxed their hands to see if they still possessed the pennies that their parents had given them before the service.

An old woman began to sing. Others joined in. A middle-aged man stood up, with the other members of the church following his example. They began to sway with the rhythm of the vocal music. Then they started to dance towards the wooden table with hands lifted up. On each down beat, people slammed their hands flat down on top of the table. When they lifted their hands I observed that they had left their offerings. For over five minutes, people kept singing and slamming down their noisy coins and silent bills.

It was then that I observed her. She was a middle-aged woman. Her clothing was clean but tattered. In her hand she was grasping a flashlight. When she reached the table, she slammed it down and left it there. She then moved on, swaying away with the other people.

I tapped the arm of the pastor next to me. "Why did she do that?"

With a large grin on his face he explained, "She is giving that flashlight to you as a gift. She noticed you stumbling in the dark tonight and thought that her flashlight could help you."

Amazed, I blurted out, "I couldn't take that light from her. It probably cost her over fifty dollars to buy it in this country. Next week, when I return home I can pick up the same flashlight for probably four dollars."

With a stern look on his face the pastor said, "Umfundisi Jim, you *will* accept her gift. If you do not, you will be hurting her feelings. But more importantly, you will be robbing her of the blessing that God wants to bestow upon her for her generosity. You are right when you said that flashlight cost her a lot of money. In fact, it probably cost her a whole month's salary to purchase it. I try to teach our Christians to give not only when they have plenty but to also be willing to give when they have only a little. The life of a Christian should be a life of giving."

*The Compassion of Missions*

As I reflect back on that night, my heart lifts a prayer to God, "Lord, thank you for using the dear lady from Mozambique to show me what true giving is. Teach me to be a generous giver like her."

# Pass-i'-on

I also find a little sentence hidden within the word *compassion*. It is "pass-i'-on."

C-o-m-**p-a-s-s-i'-o-n**

Now, I know what some of you who majored in English in college are thinking, "Doesn't Jim know that it should be 'Pass it on'?"

When I used to travel around the country doing mission conventions in different churches, I sometimes had the opportunity of going to the South. The people who live down there were delightful. Southern hospitality is what it is made out to be. While touring there, I enjoyed hearing a different style of English being spoken. I liked how they would say, "Hi, y'all" with the "y'all" really drawn out. I have decided that if some people in America can say, "Y'all," or "How's it?", I can say "pass i'on."

Romans 10:15 reads,

> How beautiful are the feet of those who bring good news. . . .

In other words, it is wonderful when believers will take the message of Christ's salvation and pass it on to others.

## Pass the chewing gum.

There were three of us. Bill was the oldest. I was the middle child and Tom was the youngest. We all loved eating candy. Red licorice, chocolate Easter bunnies, jaw breakers, Reeses peanut butter cups. As long as it was sweet, we would eat it. My favorite candy was Bazooka bubble gum. Does it bring back memories for you?

I could chew up to five Bazookas at one time. Once the pink gum became soft enough, I would begin blowing large bubbles. Bill, Tom, and I would have bubble blowing contests to see who could blow the largest bubble. Often the bubbles would pop prematurely, leaving our hair, eyebrows, and faces covered with pink gum. There were numerous times that the only way to get the gum out of our hair was to cut our hair off. But such an ordeal did not stop us from chewing gum.

Hour upon hour I would blow bubbles. By nighttime my jaws would be very sore from chewing all day long. To rest my jaws, I would take the gum out of my mouth and stick it under my bed. When my jaw was sufficiently rested, I would retrieve my already-chewed gum, stick it back in my mouth and begin chewing again.

I had read in a comic book about how one boy had blown a great big bubble and when the wind got hold of the bubble, he floated up into the sky and traveled to different places in the world. If he could do that, why couldn't I? (Childhood imagination.)

Billy, Tommy and I grew up in a home where there was not a lot of money. All our basic needs were taken care of, but there was not much left over for luxuries. If we wanted gum to chew, we had to find ways to get it ourselves.

One day at school, my pencil dropped onto the floor. As I bent over to pick it up, I happened to look under my desk. My eyes got real big. There, sticking to the underside of the desk were at least ten wads of already-chewed gum. This must have been the way the person who used my desk before me got rid of his gum. What a wonderful find! I forced one of the gum wads off the desk and proceeded to chew on it. It was hard going at first, but with time the used piece of gum got soft enough for me to continue to blow bubbles.

During this time of my life I also learned to walk around with my eyes on the ground, looking for money. One can find many interesting things by walking with your head down—a door knob, a deflated football, a broken bracelet. But sometimes I would find money. When Bill, Tom, or I found any money, we would go directly to a gum ball machine.

When I was a little boy one could buy gum balls for only one penny. That dates me, doesn't it? My brothers and I would put our penny into the machine, crank the little handle, listen to the rolling gum ball, and eagerly lift up the little door to allow the gumball to fall into one of our hands.

But we always had a problem. We rarely, if ever, found three pennies to buy three gum balls for three boys. We knew that it would not be fair for only one of us to chew the gum. So we came up with a plan that only boys could think of. We decided to take turns chewing. Since Bill was the oldest, we decided that he should have first turn. We told him that he could chew for five minutes. As he chewed, I kept my eyes on the clock. I was not willing to give him more than his allotted time. When the five minutes came to an end, I proceeded to open his mouth—as you can guess, I had to do this because he was not willing to give up the gum—stick my fingers into his mouth and retrieve what was now rightfully mine. I then stuck the pink gum into my mouth. You may not believe this, but that piece of gum would still have a little bit of sweetness left in it. As I chewed away Tommy would look longingly at me, anticipating his turn to chew. But Tommy was too young to tell time. Ten minutes would pass. "Jimmy, isn't it my turn yet?"

In between chews, I would answer, "No, Tommy, just another three minutes."

After another five minutes, "Jimmy, now?"

"No, Tommy. I still have another two minutes."

I was usually able to get in at least fifteen more minutes of chewing before Tommy would get impatient, pounce on me, and forcibly get the gum away from me. He would then stick it in his mouth to chew. I loved watching Tommy chew. In hopes of tasting some sweetness, he would chew on the gum with all his might. The veins on his skinny neck would pop out until I thought they would burst. It was so cool to see Tommy's poppy veins.

You may be wondering why I am telling you yet another dumb story. You need to understand that what we were doing as brothers was "passing it on." Gum was an important thing for us. When we were fortunate to have any, we wanted to share it with each other (even if it was grudgingly). In a way this is what we are to do as believers. We must pass on Christ's message of love and life.

## Passing on Christ's message of love and life.

How are people to understand about eternal life in Christ unless someone is willing to go and tell them . . . unless churches are willing to send preachers to preach to them . . . unless heralds of the Good News will go forth . . . unless we are willing to pass i' on.

Kum Kun San is a gentle Cambodian. Never have I heard him raise his voice in anger or frustration. At meetings, where others may be very heated over an issue, Kum Kun San would listen to all sides, and then softly share his thoughts. Always, his words were filled with love and kindness. But Kum Kun San had not always been this way. In fact, someone told me that at one time Kum Kun San was a "hot head." Within seconds his emotions could flair up, and his tongue could give a lashing that stung and hurt others deeply. What made the difference in Kum Kun San's life? How was he able to change from being a fiery hot head to being a kind, gentle man? Kum Kun San testifies that it was because of the "life changer, Jesus Christ."

Upon receiving Jesus Christ as his own personal Savior, Kum Kun San became concerned for the spiritual welfare of those whom he knew. After a Sunday evening worship service, Kum Kun San approached me and asked if we could meet.

"What do you need, Kum Kun San?"

"Look Krue Jim, I am concerned for some people I know. They are Vietnamese refugees and they are not saved. They do not know about Jesus Christ. Therefore, I would like to get your opinion about something. Do you think it would be a good idea for me to go to them and tell them about Jesus?"

"Why, that sounds like a wonderful idea."

Perhaps I should have asked more questions before I gave such a hearty endorsement. Somewhere in the process of translation, I missed out on the part where I was to be involved.

"I thought that is the way you would answer me, Look Krue Jim. I will see you tomorrow."

As he walked away from me, I sat there, wondering what I had gotten myself into. I wondered what else he had said that I had not understood.

The next day Kum Kun San arrived at the tiny, two room apartment that Roxy and I were renting. "Are you ready, Look Krue Jim?"

In a voice that portrayed my annoyance at having been "drafted" to go with him, I grunted my answer.

*The Compassion of Missions*

    Sitting behind Kum Kun San on the motorbike, I rode with him to the outskirts of Phnom Phen. As long as we traveled on blacktopped roads, the ride was bearable. But once the blacktop changed to dirt, my pleasure ride came to an abrupt end. The ruts in the road bounced me up and down, causing great discomfort even where God's provision for cushioning has been given.

    We stopped at the bank of the Mekong River. Getting off the bike, I looked at myself in its mirror. I was not prepared for what I saw. The dust from other bikes had entered into my mouth, eyes, and ears. I looked like a raccoon with the dark dust marks around my eyes. When I smiled, I could see dust specks plastered on my teeth. Have you ever seen what dust does with hair? It acts like hair gel. The combination of dust gel and wind made every strand of hair stand at attention.

    While I was desperately trying to fix my appearance, Kum Kun San was negotiating with some villagers to use one of their wooden row boats. The Vietnamese refugees we were going to visit lived on a small island in the middle of the Mekong River. After a few minutes a deal was struck.

*Pass-i'-on*

I was told where to sit in the boat and then given the following instruction, "Do not move too much. This boat is not very strong."

As the boat was pushed out into deeper waters, I fearfully grabbed onto its sides. The words "not very strong" had me worried. I did not move a muscle. About five minutes into the trip, I began to feel my underside getting wet. The boat had a leak. Silently, I began to pray for my life. I do not swim very well.

As you can guess, the Lord did spare my life. We arrived at the island where a small delegation was waiting for us. As I was helped out of the boat, I tried to cover up my wet backside with my hands. I do not think it worked. The little children of the island began pointing and they weren't pointing to the birds in the air. They were pointing directly at what I was trying to hide. Then they began to giggle. Ever see a red Chinese? I know my face was red and hot because of embarrassment. The adults were kinder than the children. Though they pointed and made a few comments to each other, they dropped the topic after a few minutes.

Kum Kun San came to my side and told me that we were being invited to get out of the hot sun and sit in one of the refugee's houses. The average monthly salary in Cambodia is approximately twenty dollars. The refugees we were visiting made only around five dollars a month. A few tree limbs, some grass and straw mats made up their house. There was no furniture. A plastic woven mat was the only "nice" thing that they had. As Kum Kun San entered into the house, those sitting on the mat got up, found some bare ground and again sat down.

"Look Krue Jim, they want you to sit on the mat. They are showing you respect."

In obedience, I sat down where I was directed.

Kum Kun San began talking to the twenty-some individuals who had gathered in the little shack. I could not keep up with the conversation since they were speaking in Khmer and Vietnamese at a very quick pace. So I just smiled.

But one can only smile for so long. I began to get antsy. It did not take long to examine everything in the house. As I already told you, they did not have much. Being bored but trying not to look bored can be a very hard thing to do. After fifteen minutes, I began to feel an itch. Now, I am not sure what you do with an itch, but I scratch. And scratch I did.

Kum Kun San looked over at me and indicated for me to stop. Have you ever had someone tell you not to scratch? I tried to obey him, but the more I tried not to scratch, the more I began to itch. What was I to do? The itch in the middle of my back was becoming unbearable. I leaned my back against the tree limb poles of the house and tried to take care of my problem inconspicuously. But my actions caught Kum Kun San's attention and once again I could read his look of disapproval. Leaning over to speak to me, he said, "Look Krue Jim, try not to scratch so much. You will embarrass these people."

With a smile on my face, I crossed my legs and sat as still as I could. Kum Kun San and the people resumed talking. Once I realized that the people were no longer paying attention to me, I relaxed my "smiley" muscles and tried to find another way of amusing myself. It was at this moment that I noticed a line of white bugs marching on my leg. In a single file they marched. This fascinated me. I began wondering where the bugs were coming from. As I watched the tiny soldiers, my itch came back. My curiosity concerning where these bugs were coming from intensified. After a few minutes, it dawned on me. My itching and the bugs crawling up my legs must be related. I then lifted the corner of my mat and there, crawling frantically, were thousands of minuscule white bugs. By this time Kum Kun San was watching what I was doing. Again he made it clear that he wanted me to behave.

I repentantly put the corner of the mat down and proceeded to watch the bugs on my pant legs. An idea then dawned on me. I began to flick the bugs off my pant legs with my fingers. One by one I "airborned" them onto the other people who were seated around me. If I had to suffer, so should they.

After a few hours we began our journey back to the city of Phnom Phen. As we drove back, Kum Kun San and I were able to talk. "Look Krue Jim, I know that those Vietnamese refugees are very poor. And I know that it is not easy to sit there with bugs crawling on you. But we should do it because we want them to know about Jesus Christ."

For the next few weeks, Kum Kun San faithfully went to visit them. Often he would bring vegetables for them to cook. When he noticed one of the girls walking around without any thongs, he went to the market and bought her some. He conducted a weekly Bible study for them, passing on God's love and message of life. In a few months' time, a family of six surrendered their hearts to Christ. I know that there was great rejoicing in Heaven. I also know that there was great rejoicing in the home of Kum Kun San. With childlike excitement, Kum Kun San was telling believers who were visiting him about the six new members in God's wonderful family.

> **I know that it is not easy to sit there with bugs crawling on you. But we should do it because we want them to know about Jesus Christ.**

# Sí

Within the great word *compassion* is finally found the tiny word, *sí*. It is not an English word, but a Spanish word meaning "yes."

### C-o-m-p-a-s-**s-í**-o-n

How appropriate that this foreign word should be found in an English word. In a way, this represents what is happening in the United States of America. No longer can one say that America is just made up of white Anglo-Saxons. Groups from every ethnic background are now calling America their home.

**Cultural diversity.**

Before I was to preach during a Sunday morning revival service, the pastor told me that he was going to introduce me first to the congregation. After the special music, he walked over to the pulpit and began to address those in attendance. "I would like to introduce our speaker. He is a Chinaman . . ."

Whatever else he may have said in his introduction did not register with me. While he was able to get a laugh from his congregation by pointing out that I was a "Chinaman," he left me feeling uncomfortable and embarrassed. Why would he even have to tell them that I am Chinese? Aren't his people intelligent enough to see that for themselves? Besides, would he stand up and introduce others as being German, or Swedish, or Italian? I do not think so.

*The Compassion of Missions*

The name "Chinaman" is a derogatory term. Its use became popular with American "Whites" years ago, when they spoke to the Chinese immigrants who had come to work on the railway lines. The word was devoid of any type of affection. Instead, it was used as a put-down.

> "I have decided that I am going to tell God that I want you as my neighbor when I get to Heaven.

Once I was the speaker at a retreat. Between speaking sessions, I decided that I was going to mingle with those who had come for the weekend. One man approached me and without any introduction, stated, "I have decided that I am going to tell God that I want you as my neighbor when I get to heaven. A few years ago, I heard a black man speak, and I told him that I was going to tell God he was going to be my neighbor as well. I plan to have a black man on one side and a Chinese man on the other."

It was not so much what he said that bothered me, but how he said it. All I could think to myself was, "Don't I have a choice in this?"

To want people to live near you only because of their skin color is not a very good reason. It was almost as if he were saying, "Look at how good I am. I am willing to lower myself and have a black man and a Chinese live next to me."

"Don't do me any favors! Maybe I don't want to live next to you," was my thought.

During the Sunday school hour at a church I was visiting, the class discussion turned to non-verbal communication. One woman raised her hand and bluntly stated, "People should look you straight in the eye when they speak to you. If they don't, it means that they are sneaky and have something they are trying to hide. I don't trust people who don't have the courage to look at me when we are talking."

*Sí*

I raised my hand to interject my comments. "In many cultures of the world, to look someone straight in the eye is a sign of rudeness. The way to show respect is to lower one's eyes when one is speaking to someone. As an oriental, this was what I was taught. It does not have to be a sign of deceit, but it can also be a sign of respect."

Under her breath, I could hear the woman say to the person sitting next to her, "Well, this is America. If foreigners want to live here, they will need to learn how to do things the right way!"

**It is imperative that the Church in America learn how to become culturally sensitive to people of different ethnic backgrounds in order to reach them with the message of Christ.**

In many churches I am repeatedly hearing the statement, "We want to reach people with the message of Christ." This is a wonderful desire to have. There are numerous people outside the fold who need to be reached with the message of salvation. The reality is that many of those who need to be reached are culturally different from the average white, middle-class backgrounds that are found in the majority of our churches. It is imperative that the Church in America learn how to become culturally sensitive to people of different ethnic backgrounds in order to reach them with the message of Christ.

**Saying "sí."**
But in order for us to reach out to others, we have to be willing to say "sí." So often believers are scared to say "yes" to God's call upon their lives. They feel that if they follow God's leading, they will not experience the best for their lives.

*The Compassion of Missions*

They are so wrong!

When Roxy and I traveled to different churches to speak about missions, I was always humored by the older ladies of the church. They can be so cute. During potluck meals they always encouraged me to try what they had cooked. If they did not think I had taken enough, they would proceed to dump more on my plate.

One old lady would pinch my cheek every time she saw me and say, "You are so cute!" (I got to the place of intentionally trying to hide from her. My cheek was getting awfully sore).

Some older ladies would come up to me, touch my arm, and exclaim, "I just touched a missionary!" (The attention was embarrassing.)

Other times they would approach me and say, "I feel so sorry for you. The sacrifices that you make to be a missionary. It must be so hard for you to go to a foreign country where the people are different, and the food is different, and the way they do things is different."

Missionaries do not need others to feel sorry for them. There is no greater joy than to be following Christ. I would agree that it is not always easy being a missionary. There are days of loneliness. After a few weeks of being in Zimbabwe, Roxy's parents celebrated their fiftieth wedding anniversary. On the day of their anniversary, Roxy's entire family was going to gather and celebrate with them. But there was no way for Roxy to go. The cost for airline tickets would have been too much for our budget. How my heart ached as I watched tears of loneliness and longing trickle from Roxy's eyes.

There are days of frustration. It saddened us to see spiritual leaders fall morally. It hurt to be criticized by nationals for not being willing to give in to their demands for money, church buildings, and cars. It was upsetting when some who testified about giving their whole heart to Christ would go to the witch doctor during times of crisis.

But I have had no regrets about following God's calling to be a missionary. What joy has filled my heart to see nationals surrender their lives to the Master. There is nothing greater than being a part of God's plan to lead others into His salvation. How my heart stirs with love for nationals who have become my dear friends.

As I have already stated, you do not have to feel sorry for missionaries. Instead, feel sorry for believers who will not say "sí" to God. They are the ones who are missing out on the adventure of walking with God. They are the ones who are missing out on the blessings that come from obedience. They are the ones who are missing out on experiencing His full joy. I contend that the most miserable people are believers who will not totally surrender to God.

## Conclusion.

Many students ask me the question, "Umfundisi, what makes a person an effective missionary for Jesus Christ?"

I usually throw the question back at to them before I give them my answer.

Many answer by saying, "To be an effective missionary for God one must have the proper training. A person should go to university and take such courses as evangelism and cross-cultural ministries, history of missions, contextualization, linguistics and cross-cultural communication." (To get on my good side, one student said, "And a person should take these course with Umfundisi Jim!")

Others have answered by stating that in order for them to be effective, they would need a "sufficient budget to start up different programs." One person shared, "give me a powerful enough computer and I will be able to accomplish anything for God!" (I wasn't sure if I was to take him seriously or not.)

Once they have had enough time to share their ideas, I give them my answer. "What makes a person and effective missionary? Even though education, money and a powerful computer may help an individual do his or her ministry more effectively, what a person really needs to be a successful and effective missionary is to be filled with God's *compassion*.